İSTANBUL - 1432 / 2011

From The Garden of Mathnawi

The Story
of the
Reed

Osman Nûri TOPBAŞ

ERKAM PUBLICATIONS

© Erkam Publications 2005 / 1426 H

Published by:
Erkam Publications
Ikitelli Organize Sanayi Bölgesi
Turgut Özal Cd. No: 117/4
Ikitelli, Istanbul, Turkey
Tel: (90-212) 671-0700 pbx
Fax: (90-212) 671-0717
E-mail: english@altinoluk.com
Web site: http://www.altinoluk.com

ISBN: 978-9944-83-136-9

Translators	:	Zeynep Alp
		Elif Kapıcı
		Zeynep Mahmout
Editor	:	Mustapha Sheikh
Cover design	:	Altinoluk Graphics
Typeset by	:	Altinoluk Graphics
Printed by	:	Erkam Printhouse

TABLE OF CONTENTS

foreword

FOREWORD

We are living in a time of materialism, in this age people are after their fleshly desires more than ever. Unfortunately, everything is valued according to its material benefit; hence there is a great need to look at the events from the windows of the heart with the eyes of wisdom. In order to do this, we have to carefully reread the works of such Sufis like Bahauddin Naqshbend, Jalaladdin Rumi, and Abdulqadir Geylani and so on.

In the past we had authored a work named "From the Garden of the Mathnawi, Tears of the Heart" being selection of chapters from Mathnawi in order to benefit from Rumi's great inheritance of spirituality. Thanks Allah, this work attracted the attention of Muslims and their praise. It proved that the solutions of Sufis are still very much effective in the modern world. Hence in order to benefit from the reviving breath of Rumi, we supplied with the readers another *Jug of Water* from the ocean of Rumi.

It should be once more emphasized that Rumi is not only important for a particular nation, he is a very important source of illumination for all the nations of the world. His books are the ocean of wisdom and Divine Realities. Rumi went through to the depths of man's heart; he understood the reality of man and supplied us with remedies of continuous beauty.

It is very rare to find other works of Sufism like Mathnawi, which can so successfully explaining the spiritual truths, by using stories he made the difficult subject of spiritual life easily understandable to the seekers of gnosis.

Allah Almighty out of his grace gave us an opportunity to prepare this work, benefiting from his works and spiritual world. I claim no credit to myself in this work except the role of typist who typed it.

May Allah give success to this modest work and make it a continuous charity (al-Sadaqah al-Jariyah) for me and as well as for those who helped in its preparation. May Allah accept our sincere intentions and make it a window of light for those who seek for the truth and solve their spiritual problems. Amin!

Success comes only from Allah.

Osman Nûri Topbaş
03 July 2009

The Story the of Ney

THE STORY OF THE NEY[1] IN THE MATHNAWI

𝒯he *Ney* (flute) that is mentioned in Rûmî's stories in fact represents the perfect man (Insân-i Kâmil).[2] The stages a reed goes through from the reed bed to becoming a *ney* portrays the maturation of a human being, a representation of the steps of purifying the *nafs* (lower self) and refining the heart.

In the same way that the *ney* is severed from the reed bed and this separation causes it to lament in pain, the perfect man, who has come from the realm of souls and enters a body made out of clay, known as the cage made of flesh, yearns for the original realm. Through this yearning a human being goes through ascetic discipline (*riyâda*), meditation (*murâqaba*),

---

1. The ney (also nai, nye, nay) is a light-brown flute that figures prominently in Middle Eastern music. In some of these musical traditions, it is the only wind instrument used. It is a very ancient instrument, with depictions of ney players appearing on wall paintings in the Egyptian pyramids and actual neys being found in the excavations at Ur. This indicates that the ney has been played continuously for 4,500–5,000 years, making it one of the oldest musical instruments still in use. It is a forerunner of the modern flute. (Translator)
2. Insan-i Kamil, a human being that has reached spiritual completeness in every way. (Translator)

reflection (*tafakkur*), Divine love and tribulations until he reaches maturity and finds perfection.

The *ney* that is removed from the reed bed is carefully cut by the craftsman. Then the inside is removed and the reed is left to dry. Later, holes are burnt through and rings are placed at the top and bottom. After being left in this state for some time, when the *neyzen*[3] breathes into it, the *ney* starts to send out beautiful sounds, as well as wonder and wisdom, in accordance with the listener's spiritual level.

A human being goes through similar stages on the path to perfection. Perfect men are chosen from among other men according to certain criteria. One of the most important attributes of the Prophets is that they are "chosen". They are cleansed of mortal bonds and preoccupations through various methods of nurturing. On the path of special religious training which is called sayr u suluk, they face hardships, misfortunes and trials, which are necessary to gain patience, and they mature by following the path of "revelation". Finally, they become instruments in which Allah's art, wisdom and might are manifested. People yield to the spiritual wisdom that emanates from them and they start to proceed in the direction of unity with the beloved.

A figurative story is narrated in the Mawlawi[4] sources about the first appearance of the *ney*, this instrument that shares the same fate as humans, and its use:

The Prophet entrusted a drop of the ocean of secrets and wisdom that had been bestowed upon him by Allah Almighty to 'Alî (ﷺ), who is known as the *Gate of Knowledge*, strictly

---

3. The musician who plays the *ney*.
4. The Sufi order that follows Mawlana Jalaladdin Rumi.

warning him not to reveal these secrets. Ali (ؑ) could not bear what had been entrusted to him and was crushed by its great weight. He took to the desert. He revealed what he had kept inside him down a black well. In time, the well flowed with water. Reeds started to grow in the water that overflowed from the well. A shepherd, realizing that these reeds made beautiful sounds when the wind blew through them, cut one and made a *ney*. The sound coming from this *ney* is so heartfelt and emotional that everyone fell in love with the deep, poignant and soulful tunes. They started laughing and crying at the sound. Soon this shepherd's reputation spread and the Arab tribes started to gather around to listen to him. (Ahmed Eflâkî, Âriflerin Menkıbeleri, II, 440)

Hence, Mawlânâ's *Mathnawi* is the written form of these pleasant tunes and the mystery they carry within them. For this reason, those who read the *Mathnawi* find themselves forced to admit that as the meanings deepen, they carry manifold mysteries and wisdom. Mawlânâ, who observed the profound ocean contained in a small drop, exhibits this to us in accordance with our capacity, and there are great seas and even oceans in these verses, each of which is considered to be a small drop. Although the *Mathnawi* carries deep meanings and wisdom, Mawlânâ is lamenting the fact that he cannot explain his secrets as he wishes. In this regard, contemplating the first recipient of *Mathnawi*, he says: *"I wrote this Mathnawi for Husâmeddîn!"*

Another time, pointing out the infinity of Allah's knowledge and wisdom, he says: *"I had the Mathnawi written down as an abstract. If I were to further interpret the mysteries and the wisdom, forty camels would have had difficulty carrying them."*

15

To explain the inability of most humans to grasp the spiritual meanings in this work, a sage who dearly loved Mawlâna said:

"We listened to the cries of Rûmî's ecstasy. It is impossible to see the depths of the sea of passion that he dived into. We only see what has come to the surface from the depths. We only acquire the cries of love that he has uttered, but not his love. It is this alone that we are trying to explain while we lisp. Only Rûmî has been able to dive into the sea of peace. We are left with the sounds that come through the storm of his ecstasy. Alas! We think he is Mawlânâ!"

The Spiritual Echo (sada) of the Perfect Man According to the Mathnawi

THE SPIRITUAL ECHO (SADA) OF THE PERFECT MAN
ACCORDING TO THE MATHNAWI
(The Crying of the Ney)

*T*he **Mathnawi:** *"If you were to pour the sea of sustenance into a pitcher, how much would it hold? Only as much as it is capable of… that is, the portion of every creature that has been preordained for them alone…."* (v.1: 20)

It is Allah Almighty Who preordains a sufficient sustenance for all creatures. It is absurd to be ambitious in securing this sustenance. In a hadith[5] it is said: *"Like death, sustenance will find each person."* (Ibn Hibbân, *Sahîh*, VIII: 31). This means no creature's life will come to an end before it uses up the sustenance that has been preordained for it. Like other things that are predestined by Allah Almighty, sustenance is connected to means; effort and action are a necessity, a responsibility and are mandatory in reaching these means. But to think that the result, which is the sustenance, is from oneself is great heedlessness. Means produce results according to their relevance. Therefore, the wise human being knows that sustenance comes from Allah

---

5. *Hadîth:* a saying of the Prophet Muhammad (ﷺ)

Almighty Who has created the means; it comes through His predestination, not through the means that one is pursuing.

He is the One who sends sustenance. We should seek the Razzâq[6] who sends us this sustenance. In the Qur'ân it is said: *"...We ask not of thee a provision: We provide for thee..."* (Tâhâ, 20: 132)

The Mathnawi: *"The pitchers, the eyes of the covetous, will never become full. And if the mother of pearl is not content it will never be impregnated with pearls."* (v1: 21)

There is ambition in each and every creature, to varying degrees, but it is certainly there. If you give the same toy to two children, one will envy what the other has only to the degree of their innate inclination to envy. It is only possible to minimize this inclination through training the nafs. For this reason in the Qur'ân it is said: "But those will prosper who purify themselves (purifying from foul inclinations)" (A'lâ, 87: 14). The first condition of peace and felicity in society is to adhere to what Allah has preordained for us. This preordination is a requirement of the destiny that is absolute and unconditional (*qadar-i mutlak*). Destiny is an ocean of secrets. It is not possible to be aware of all the wisdom that is hidden within. So it is a necessity to submit to Allah's will and to have faith in the wisdom of this will. Those who cannot obtain this state will be ruined in the whirls of the pit of hell, where all sorts of desires overflow.

The Mathnawi: *"The person who is relieved from the sensuality and selfishness of his nafs and is freed from the shroud of the ego through Divine love is entirely cleansed*

---

6. One of Allah's beautiful names which means the One who Provides Sustenance for all Creation.

from covetousness and from all kinds of disgrace and ugliness." (v.1: 22)

Those who nurture their souls and reach the pleasure of *imân*[7] are free from the worries of life and fortune. They become instruments and opportunities by which the Lord Almighty's love can be reached. But this is not a maturity that can be easily reached. Through patience, determination, worship, prayer and the struggle against the nafs, one needs to show constant perseverance. Even the earth is beautified with the blessings of spring because it bears the difficulties of winter. The mother of pearl is blessed with the happiness of the presence of the pearl in its bosom through this endeavor.

The Mathnawi: *"Our body, which has been created from earth, soars to the skies through love and becomes sublime."* (v.1: 25)

The human body belongs to the earth. In this respect it is no different from other beings in creation. Like all of creation, humans are created from the earth; they feed on what they can attain from the earth and they are a transformed form of the earth. In the end they return to the earth and perish. But our spiritual qualities belong to Allah Almighty. In a verse in the Qur'ân it is said: "...and breathed into him of My spirit..." (Hijr, 15: 29; Sâd, 38: 72). The Lord Almighty has bestowed His servants with certain capabilities and inclinations so that they can be elevated towards Him. Those who can eliminate perverse, human tendencies and enter the path of perfection start to advance towards a Divine union.

Rûmî said:

---

7. *Îmân* means belief, an adherence to Islam.

"Do not care for nurturing the body in excess. In the end, it is a sacrifice that will be given to the earth. Nurture your soul for it is your soul that will be honoured and reach noble places."

"Give little of the oily or sweet things to your body, because those who feed on it to excess fall into the whims of the nafs and are disgraced in the end."

"Give your soul spiritual nourishment. Give it mature thinking, fine judgment and spiritual provision so it can go to its destination as an eternal traveller that is strong and powerful."

The Mathnawi: *Those who are only familiar with their own language and soul would be speechless and silent when removed from the people who understand their expressions and resolve, even if they were to know hundreds of languages and songs."* (v.1: 28)

The Prophet Muhammad (ﷺ) said: *"Talk to people according to their level of understanding"* (Bukhârî, 'Ilm, 49). Regardless of their nobility, words and expressions that are beyond the listener's comprehension are of no benefit. From this point of view, people who witness the deep and refined feelings that come from the soul must also be people of the soul, because being with people who are immersed in the corruption of sins blinds the eyes of the body and the soul. Words that are spent on senseless and ignorant people are wasted. These are like rare flowers that bloom on the edges of sidewalks, condemned to be trampled and perish.

Although Mawlânâ took a path that would bring his great work of the *Mathnawi* into existence so that it would be beneficial to both the common and the distinguished (khawâs) people, he said: *"I will die longing for a man of insight..."*

On the other hand, there has to be mutual love for any teaching to bring about the desired outcome in the respondent. Love is such a magical instrument of influx that through that channel, without even turning to speech, it can pass from one soul to another. It is for this reason that Sufis use love for all kinds of teaching and guidance.

True friendship for the sake of Allah consists of two separate bodies living in one heart. In other words, friends become two hands that wash each other. Just like the *Muhâjirûn* and the *Ansâr*[8]...

The Mathnawi: *"When the freshness of the rose has gone and the rose garden has entered the season of autumn, the beautiful songs and laments of the nightingale will not be heard."* (v.1: 29)

A human's affection for another and the fruit of this affection, which is tender conversation, resembles the encounter of the rose and the nightingale. In general, words and thoughts that are uttered by humans are suited to the listener's aptitude and spiritual needs. The one talking is the heart, while the tongue acts as translator. Expressions are almost like a heartsick tune from the *ney*. The listener is the person who is playing the *ney*. If the person playing the *ney* is an amateur, then that assembly is similar to a rose garden that has entered autumn.

The Mathnawi: *"Those who distance themselves from their mortal being and are free of the selfish nafs -namely those who are familiar with and are attached to immortals- are*

---

8. *Muhâjirûn*: The Companions of the Prophet who emigrated from Mecca to Medina due to extreme pressure. *Ansâr*: The people of Medina who embraced the *Muhajirûn*.

23

the fortunate ones. Pity those who are living but sitting with the dead and are spiritually dead themselves ..." (v.1: 1513)

Allah Almighty says: "O ye who believe! Fear Allah and be with those who are true (in word and deed)" (Tawba, 9: 119). True happiness is possible through reinforcing high morality, which is attained through *fayz*[9] and the spirituality that emanates from the souls of people who are close to Allah. Their graceful demeanour, through togetherness, which is a prerequisite of affection, emanates and matures people who pass from one soul to another. The Companions of the Prophet are the best examples of this. These people, whose past was full of savagery, burying their daughters alive, not caring for justice or law, reached the highest peaks of morality and virtue through their love and closeness to the Prophet Muhammad. (ﷺ) In degrees, people who are close to Allah are all in the same situation.

This situation is expressed in Rûmî's language as such:

"O friend, do not despair because you have not reached the beloved Prophet and are not able to reap similar benefits... Be with the faithful, who are his followers, you will receive your sustenance according to your aptitude and inclination."

The greatest spiritual disaster is to go against Allah's order "...sit not thou in the company of those who do wrong!" (An'âm, 6: 68) and being with those who live under the influence of their *nafs*. Feeling affection towards these people is the cause of a devastating loss that occurs through the reflection of all kinds of negativism from heart to heart.

---

9. Spiritual power that emanates from a person and inspires greater enlightenment.

Those who are always with the virtuous become one of them and those who are with the oppressors become oppressors and partners to their oppression and crime. Mawlânâ explains this truth in another place as follows:

"Keep company with people of spirituality, receive kindness and benevolence as well as spiritual strength; stay young, robust and healthy with Divine love."

"This soul that is in the flesh, if it is unaware of love, is like a wooden sword in its sheath. As long as that wooden sword is in the sheath, it will be presumed worthy, useful; when it is drawn from its sheath it is only worth burning."

"If it is of wood, go and look for another sword. If it is of diamonds, then spring forward with joy. A diamond sword is the weapon of the saints. To see this is alchemy for you. It is a spiritual strength..."

"Whether you are a very hard stone or a piece of marble, if you find a man of soul, you will become a jewel, namely an emerald, a diamond. Place the love of those pure saints in your heart. Do not give your heart to anyone except to the love of the wise."

The Mathnawi: *"When the voice of love came to the dead, souls started fluttering; the dead raised their heads from the tombs of their bodies."* (v.4: 840)

The Prophets and the saints are an elixir. With them hardened, lifeless souls are revived and invigorated.

The Mathnawi: *"O desirous human! Know this: the soul is the greatest work of Divine mercy. Other things are like shadows of this great work."* (v.4: 1362)

"A river flows amongst the trees. In its clear waters you will see the reflection of the trees on both sides."

"The reflections in the water are imaginary gardens. The true gardens are within the soul, because the soul is the place of the Divine gaze." (v.4: 1364-1365)

One should not forget that the heart is a place for the Divine gaze. According to a tradition, Allah Almighty said: *"The skies and the earth cannot contain me; only the heart of one of my believing servants."* (Ajlûnî, *Kashfu'l-Khafâ*, II: 195)

The Mathnawi: *"Saints have such power bestowed upon them by the Lord Almighty that they turn back the arrow which has left the bow from its course."*

"When a saint is troubled regarding an incident that takes place, with the Lord's hand of power, he will close the door of reason that generated the incident." (v.1: 1669-1670)

The value and attainment possessed by the people who are close to Allah are described in a *hadîth qudsî*[10] as follows:

"Whoever is belligerent against my saintly servant, I will declare war against him. My servant cannot come closer to me with anything more delightful than the fard[11] I have enjoined on him. My servant continues to draw closer to Me with the nawâfil[12]until I love him. When I love my servant, I become (as if I am) his tongue that talks, his heart that thinks, his ears that hear, his eyes that see, his hands that grasp and his feet that walk. I will give whatever he wants from me by all means. I will help him when he asks

---

10. Word of Allah that is not written in the Qur'an but revealed by the Prophet himself.
11. *Fard*: Obligatory religious duties in Islam.
12. Nawâfil: Voluntary acts of worship

for help; I will protect him if he seeks protection in me..."
(Bukhârî, *Riqâq*, 38)

In another *hadîth* the Messenger of Allah (ﷺ) said:

"There are some of Allah's servants who are neither messengers nor martyrs, but on the Day of Judgment the Messengers and Martyrs will look at them with a longing because of their status with their Lord."

The Companions of the Prophet asked: *"Who are these and what kind of good deeds have they done? Let us know, O Messenger of Allah, so we can show them affection and closeness."*

The Messenger of Allah (ﷺ) replied: *"These are such people that, in spite of not having any ties of family, trade or business, they love each other only for the sake of Allah. I swear by Allah that their faces are alight and they are upon radiant pulpits. They have no fear at a time when people are in fear, they are not sad at a time when people are sad."* And he then read the following verses from the Qur'ân:

"Behold! Verily on the friends of Allah there is no fear, nor shall they grieve; Those who believe and (constantly) guard against evil; For them are glad tidings, in the life of the present and in the Hereafter; no change can there be in the words of Allah. This is indeed the supreme felicity." (Yûnus, 10: 62-64) (Hâkim, *Mustadrak*, IV: 170)

Mawlânâ comments on these verses:

"Allah sent Messengers and saints to the world as a mercy. For this reason they will give good council to people without fail. For those who do not take heed they pray and

27

say: 'O Allah! Have mercy on these; do not close the door of benevolence on them!'"

"Come to your senses and listen to the advice of the saints. Listen and break free from fear and sadness, find spiritual comfort and reach security!"

"Before losing the opportunity and falling into doubt, hold onto the perfect man who has shunned the deceits of this passing world and completely surrendered himself to Allah so that you will be free of the seditions of these corrupt times that are close to the end!"

"The words of the saints resemble a river that is lucid, pure and full of an elixir. While there is still an opportunity, drink from it heartily so that spiritual flowers and roses will blossom in your soul."

The Mathnawi: *"The Lord Almighty disclosed His names and attributes to Adam. But, it was through Adam that He proclaimed these names to others."* (v.1: 1943)

"Harvest Allah's light whether through Allah or through a perfect man. Drink the wine of love whether from a jar or from a goblet." (v.1: 1944)

"The one who has seen the candle that takes its light from another has indeed seen the actual candle."

"Thus, if that candle's light is transferred to a hundred candles and hundreds of candles are lit by that candle, the person who sees the light of the last candle will have actually seen the light of the first."

"Whether you take the light of hidâya[13], the light of love, from the last candle, or whether you take it from

---

13. The right path of Islam.

Him, the candle of life, there is no difference between them." (v.1: 1947-1949)

On account of the reasons listed above, the title *warathat al-anbiyâ*, Inheritors of the Prophets, is given to those special people who, by developing their comprehension and perception, have reached subtle understanding and the joy of faith (*imân*), have attained perfection within their souls along with their outer appearance through spiritual manifestations in the way of *zuhd /ascetism) and *taqwâ*.

For those who have not seen the Prophet (ﷺ) and his followers, the people close to Allah who are working to eliminate the impediments that arise from their *nafs* on the way to Allah Almighty are actual and concrete examples that can be followed. The exemplary lifestyles of these sages and their guidance are the ultimate manifestations of prophetic morals that reach beyond time.

Because they are like magnets, a core of attraction for those who have *imân* and aptitude, they are hubs of love and kindness for all segments of society, for they have been endeared to all by Allah Almighty. As stated in the following verse:

"As for those who believe and do right actions, the All-Merciful will bestow His love on them." (Maryam, 10: 96)

The Lament
of the Reed
(Longing in the Heart of the Perfect Man)

THE LAMENT OF THE REED
(Longing in the Heart of the Perfect Man)

While on a journey from the world of the souls to eternity, man finds himself on an adventure that not only presents conflicts but which is also filled with boundless joys and anticipation. The most arduous and dangerous phase of the journey is the time spent in this world. The adventure of life in this world is like a narrow corridor that stretches between the crib and the coffin, and it certainly is a difficult journey. The outcome of this journey will be either infinite happiness and blessings or unfathomable disappointment and loss.

People turn a blind eye to many truths; most importantly of all, they ignore what is beyond the beyond because of the veils of heedlessness that have been pulled over their eyes. Those who live without comprehending their position, duties and responsibilities in this temporary abode feel as if they are immortal and that death is distant, especially if they do not learn from the wisdom of asking and the contemplation of questions such as: "Who am I? Where did I come from and why? What is the truth of the existence of this world? ". They rebel against their mortality. Their yearning for eternity diminishes and thus they are at a disadvantage when preparing for the Afterlife. They condemn themselves to a life of deception, enraptured by the glitter of this world. However, the most important part of spiritual intuition and maturity for the human being starts with solving the riddle of the earth and the grave. Unless minds and hearts are devoted to what lays under the ground, it is not possible for them to access the realm of the grave.

The knowledge that is needed for drawing the road map to eternity and infinity, for uncovering the secret of death, belongs only to our Lord. The voice that provides the most satisfactory answer for this, that which provides the most certain and blessed guidance, belongs to the Prophets and their successors. Therefore, those friends of Allah who have been blessed with such Divine knowledge in their hearts, and who continue the duties of the Prophets, live in Divine elation, with the joy of being selected to awaken the heedless. They manifest wisdom and set examples, both real and metaphorical, in thousands of different ways and fashions, thus helping the Divine secrets become something more than a mere account of information, enabling them to penetrate the heart. In this respect, the first eighteen couplets of Mawlânâ Jalâluddîn Rûmî written as a prologue to his *Mathnawi* include the profoundest meanings of wisdom as well as many secrets. There are many converts to Islam who have chosen to become Muslims merely due to the impression of the secrets these couplets left on them.

Rûmî's heart is one that is intoxicated, burning with the fire of love for the Lord, burning with a thirst that keeps rising, which cannot be quenched. In fact, he never ceases, not even for one moment, to yearn and endeavor to be one with the Beloved. However, some of Rûmî's contemporaries were unable to comprehend his wisdom and the secrets born of an atmosphere of love; they talked behind his back in a number of ways. Without ever understanding his suffering, his efforts or the state of never-ending love, enthusiasm and intoxication, they caused him harm. Rûmî suffered because of their lack of understanding and tried to explain the yearning that exists in the heart of the perfect man through the lamenting song of the reed. As a matter of fact, Rûmî began his writing: "My secret is not separate from my laments; in fact, it is from my laments", and he went on to bid the reader to "Listen!"

What we should do then is to lend an ear to the laments of Rûmî and his order to "Listen!" Rûmî, the sultan of love, succinctly says:

Listen to the song of the reed,

How it wails with the pain of separation:

Ever since I was taken from my reed bed

My woeful song has caused men and women to weep.

In other words, the reed is saying: "I used to be in a reed-bed. Both my roots and my heart were established in the water and in the ground. When I was there, I would sway gracefully from one side to another with every wind that blew my way. But one day, they cut me out of the reed bed. They sucked my body dry with the love of fire and then they scorched me and cut holes in me. They opened many wounds in my skin. And then they put me in the hands of one with a mighty breath. His warm breath of love passed through me. This breath drew out of me all there was but love. From that time on, I have cried out of love and my laments have continued to rise. My laments and cries, in truth, tell of the infinite, Divine secrets that are contained within me. They sing only of the truth and happiness that I have attained.

In other words, my secrets are expressions hidden in the form of sounds that are in turn metaphorical revelations of my secrets. However, those who have not attained the light that will let them see past my secrets - because their eyes have no clear sight of the truth and their ears are rusty - are not in a state to understand the truths of which I tell."

In the *Mathnawi* Mawlânâ Rûmî desires that those who listen to the reed attain Divine feelings after hearing its lamentation.

The original home of the reed, that is, the reed bed, is a symbol that refers to the union of human beings with Allah in eternity before coming to this world. Also, the fact that Allah Almighty has said of human beings in the Qur'an: "I have made him perfectly and breathed into him of My Spirit" means that the world of souls has in it a secret from Allah; it is said that those who are perfect men and those with spiritual insight are cognizant of this, burning with the yearning to become one with their Lord throughout their life.

Commentators on the *Mathnawi* interpret its commencement with the command *"Bishnav!"* (*Listen!*) as Rûmî's attempt to show that the act of listening is a complement to the Qur'ân's initial command *"Iqra!"* (Read!). He is essentially asking the reader to "Listen to the word of the Lord! Listen to the secrets! Listen to the truth hidden within you!"

The *Mathnawi* is like a bowl of dew that has been gathered from the truths and the secrets of the Qur'an for the people of the heart. Moreover, Rûmî begins his work with the 'b' of 'bishnav'; this is also the symbol for the *basmalah* (the phrase uttered by Muslims at the beginning of any act and which means 'In the name of Allah'). As a matter of fact, the letter 'b' was actually used at the beginning of writings, letters, and treatises to symbolize the *Basmalah* in Islamic culture. This practice finds its roots in the following words of our master 'Alî: "All that is in the Qur'an is in *Sûrat al-Fâtiha* and all that there is in *Sûrat al-Fâtiha* is in the *Basmalah;* all that is in the *Basmalah* is in the letter *'b'* found at the beginning of the word."

The first eighteen couplets of the *Mathnawi* contain a world of secrets which testify to the intellectual subtlety and skill of Rûmî and also to the profundity of his words. It is for this reason that the prologue of the *Mathnawi* is explained couplet by couplet, word by word, or even letter by letter in many interpretations. In other words, these eighteen couplets are as important to the *Mathnawi*, a work that is comprised of more than twenty-six thousand couplets, as the *Sûrat al-Fâtiha* is to the Qur'ân. The first eighteen couplets were recorded by Rûmî himself, while he composed the rest to be written down by his devoted follower Husâmaddîn Jalabî.

In Rûmî's view, the reed is the symbol of the perfect man who has rid himself of the desires of his egotistical self, who has annihilated his ego, and now, self-abnegated, is full of Divine love. The woe of the reed is due to its separation from the reed bed, its homeland. Likewise, man has been exiled from the eternal world, sent into this world as a trial in which he is separated from the sacred tekke (lodge) of Allah. Therefore, the human soul mourns its separation from Allah. Man, until he reaches complete fulfillment, will continue to burn, with a yearning for the happiness and serenity of the world of souls as he struggle in exile through pain, sickness and trouble. Throughout his entire life he will wail, either in silence or out loud, with a longing for a journey towards the world of union with the Beloved without being deceived by all that exists in this temporary place, a place where man exists only as an exile;

his soul, and perhaps his body, a total stranger. Just like the woeful songs of the reed.

Man is also imprisoned in a cage that is his body. The desires of both his ego and his flesh are obstacles on the way to becoming one with his Lord. Having been confined in the cage that is his body, the heart of he who is a perfect man in love with the Lord always burns with the fire of separation and longing.

The result is that those who are overcome with the love of Allah are like fish in the sea. Even the sea of love in which they immerse themselves cannot quench their thirst. However, those who deny themselves this profound love are like those who are heedless enough to remain starving while sitting in front of a grand dinner table arrayed with thousands of dishes. Each day, they struggle in vain for a life that is as dim and dark as night. Immature souls such as these are left unaware and devoid of the Divine blessings that are bestowed upon pure and complete souls. This is true to the extent that words and meaning can make no impression on such people.

In summary, in the eighteen couplets which start with "Listen!" and end with the lines: "For a lower man, the stage of the perfect man is too lofty, so cut a long story short and say goodbye to him" apart from there being conveyed a general meaning, there are many great secrets. Perceiving an entire ocean in a single drop, Rûmî presents us with oceans to contemplate in each of his couplets.

In fact, Rûmî says, "I want a heart that is ripped apart to tell of the troubles of yearning and longing", thus expressing the fact that only those in love, who burn with the fire to become one with the Beloved, can truly understand him. To understand

this, one should think about the following example of how Rûmî perceives the perfect man:

"It was at night and I had gone out for a walk. I saw a man looking around with a lantern in his hand and I asked him: "What are you looking for at this time of the night?"

He said: "I am looking for a man"

I said to him: "Poor soul! You are wasting your time. I too left my homeland in search for him but have been unable to. Go back home. Go back to your sleep and enjoy it. You are looking for him in vain. You will not be able to find him anywhere."

The poor man looked at me with sad eyes: "I too understand this. But I continue, for I enjoy looking for him."

There is a longing to seek out the perfect man, the most dignified of all that has been created. The moment that this search transforms into a passion, one finds that for which he is looking. Otherwise, pure knowledge and searching without struggle can yield nothing. This is because love starts with struggle. To be able to go beyond the ocean of life and come together with the beloved is only possible with the blessings that come with the struggle of love and intoxication. Hearts without Divine Love are burdens on people's chests; they are heavy loads caught up in the whirlpools of the ocean of life; in the end they will be drowned and destroyed.

Hearts are like fish. Whether fish live or die depends on their existence in the sea and feeding on the food provided. Once the fish leaves the sea, its life ends and it dies. The heart too, if left without remembrance and love of Allah, becomes like a fish out of water. It becomes heedless and is ruined in the grasp of one's lower self (nafs). It remains unaware and imperceptive when confronted by the manifestations of Divine greatness and wisdom.

May Allah Almighty make us of those who listen to the Divine call of perfect men, from those who are able to see their wisdom and secrets; may He make us of those who burn with a yearning of love and intoxication for being one with Him just as the reed and may He lead us, finally, to Himself. Âmîn!

The Essentials Of Friendship In The Mathnawi

THE ESSENTIALS OF FRIENDSHIP IN THE MATHNAWI

The Mathnawi: *"Man is almost consisted of eye-vision, that is spiritual perception; the rest is (worthless) skin. The real eye on the other hand is the one that can see the Beloved. If the eye cannot see the Beloved do not consider it as an eye."* (v.1: 1406)

The eye is a window that opens to the world of thought and feeling. In reality, everything one sees, whether good or bad, generates reflections and associations in the heart and mind.

The first step in contemplation and deep reflection is to look around with an eye of consideration. Allah Almighty invites His servants to acquire a perception that is the means for grasping the meanings of these considerations; in various verses He says: *"Do they not look ... at the camel... at the clouds... at the rain... at the mountains... at the herbage that dies in the winter and returns to life in the spring or at the works of the people who lived aforetime?"*

In the Qur'ân, after mention of Allah Almighty's blessings, humans are addressed several times as "those with comprehension and vision" and are expected to contemplate the universe with perception. Many similar verses decree that humans look at the universe not with empty or hollow eyes, but with a perceptive eye in order to comprehend the wisdom of it. In such a manner, many verses ask: *"Do they not contemplate? Do they not think? Do they not comprehend?"* Those who observe the universe with such perception apprehend its Creator and His art, which, in proportion to human potency, leaves the mind helpless.

The universe is a source of Divine joy. This work of art, which is called the human being, is the manifestation of Divine joy. The eyes that see and the hearts that perceive do not perceive or see anything but Divine joy.

Human beings should raise their heads at dawn and look at the rising sun, observing the colourful scenes of the horizon. How can we, who are filled with admiration at the sight of a painting by an artist, stay apathetic and impassive before the exquisite pictures that are continuously drawn by the Divine artist, which are observed wherever we turn? Look at the tulip or violet. Where did they find these colours in the black earth? What about the red mulberry? Look at the blue and the pink of the flower that trembles under the sunlight and all the other beautiful things that we cannot even begin to count. There is a wonderful exhibition all around for a heart that has emotional depth. Look at the grace of the flower, the dance of the bee and the butterfly, look at the moth that throws itself at the fire, the laments of a nightingale and then turn and look at yourself. All of this, all the beauty, consists of a spark that comes from the reflection that seeps from the beauty of Lord Almighty.

The sun that illuminates at dawn brings us the tidings of a new day, as if saying: "Wake up!" and brings us into an atmosphere of reckoning: "Once again this morning you have been presented with a new page from the book of life. How will you fill this page which will be brought in front of you on the Day of Judgment? What are you planning to prepare for the fearful day when you will hear the order: "Read your book! Today your *nafs* is a sufficient reckoner against you."

When the evening closes, the skies turn red and then with every wave they are painted black; the night talks to humans with poise and says: "Another day has passed. You are a step closer to death. There is no need for useless lamentation. You cannot bring back the passing day, however much you strive. Now you will surrender yourself to the arms of sleep, a sibling of death. What did you do? What should you have done? Put whatever you have and have not done in front of you and think! Maybe you will never see the lights of the morning again."

The souls who turn towards the universe with contemplation and reverence will finally find Allah Almighty as the truly beloved and the genuine companion. The greatest helper of a human in regards to admonition and wisdom is submission to the revelation which directs contemplation and reverence, and establishing a true friendship with the pious ones who have become companions of Allah Almighty! Calling these pious people "companions" is a metaphor. Although true companionship means orienting towards Allah with devotion, it is a requirement of human weakness to befriend those who are close to Him and to metaphorically actualize the absolute love and friendship as a first stage of reaching Allah Almighty. This is because spiritual elevation can only be achieved in stages; it cannot be sudden. Therefore, on this journey, it is imperative to have human friendships, which are an indispensable phase of reaching Allah's companionship.

In the following verses Rûmî explains this matter further:

"If you fall into despair because of loneliness and the lack of a mind to consult, seek the shade of a friend who belongs to the sun of truth."

"Go, quickly find yourself one of His friends; if you do so, Allah will become your companion and helper."

"Seclusion and solitude can only be towards strangers but not towards the friend. The fur is for the winter not for the spring."

"When a healthy mind unites with another healthy mind trained with revelation, it strengthens, the light from it increases and it will see the way clearly."

"The nafs likes to be with another nafs just for its selfish desire of fulfilment, and so the darkness on that path increases, the truth becomes invisible."

The Mathnawi: *"O heart! Go where they shine towards you, and where there are mature people close to you so that they can act as armour for you against afflictions."*

"They will pardon your wrong deeds and give you a place within their souls." (v.2: 2576-2577)

Punishing incorrect actions in order to prevent them from happening again is a standard rule of law in all judicial systems. The Sharî'ah also prefers this route of prevention. The Sufis, while not welcoming or rationalizing such behaviour, use a method to compensate for corrupt behaviour, evaluating the perpetrator of such actions as a person being unable to protect himself from falling into erroneous behaviour. They see the person as a bird with a broken wing. Instead of punishing them immediately they turn to treatment options, just as in medicine.

No doctor would scold a patient and ask: "Why didn't you protect yourself from having a car accident" or "...from getting a cold?" On the contrary, the doctor will accept his responsibility to treat the patient. Sufis treat flawed people in the same way that doctors treat their patients. Broken objects are taken to a repairman. The skill of the repairman is relative to the perfection of the object that was broken.

Mawlânâ Rûmî states this truth as follows: "They will pardon your ill-doings and give you a place within their souls."

Mathnawi: *"The penetrating intellect, through separation from its friends, (becomes) like an archer whose bow is broken."* (v.3: 3693)

In Islam the intellect is called *'aql al-nâqis* (the deficient intellect). It means that the intellect on its own is not sufficient to arrive at what is good or to discover Allah. This truth is confirmed by the fact that Allah Almighty sent Prophets to human beings, creatures that He has endowed with intellect. The intellect is the prerequisite for man to be held responsible. In all judicial systems a person who commits murder without any intellectual capacity is pardoned. Such people are not punished. Offenders who are punished receive such treatment because their intellect and conscience are deemed to be intact. Even this shows that the intellect does not have the perfection needed to protect a human from wrongdoings.

Because of this deficiency, one intellect should be buttressed by other intellects. The rule that "two minds are better than one" demonstrates the necessity of consultation with those who are competent and qualified. Consultation is ordered in many verses of the Qur'ân so that self-improvement as well as societal may be facilitated: *"...and consult them in affairs (of the moment)!.."*

(Âl 'Imrân, 3: 159) *"…those who (conduct) their affairs by mutual Consultation …"* (Shûrâ 42: 38)

The Mathnawi: *"Whoever you see engaged in search of Allah, O son, become his friend and submit yourself to him."*

"…through being a neighbour of the seekers of Allah you yourself will become a seeker, and through them you yourself will become a conqueror." (v.3: 1446-1447)

In Turkish there is a saying: "The grape will ripen when together with other grapes." Sufis say "The (emotional, intellectual, spiritual) state is contagious" which means "a condition or a state passes from one person to another". Your state will change according to the person you love and with whom you spend your time. For this reason Allah Almighty says in the Qur'ân: *"…be with those who are true (in word and deed)"* (Tawba, 9: 119). A person receives a share of the fate of those whom they love and to whom they have mutual inclinations and feelings. Being together with the pious brings about a positive effect on the improvement of a person.

The Mathnawi: *"Know this for sure: in the end all of the mortal and dishonest companions and false lovers will become adversaries against you. They will become the foes that slay."*

"…whereas you will be left in the tomb, lamenting and beseeching Allah and (crying), 'Do not leave me (here) alone'" (v.5: 1523-1524)

Humans have a closeness and heartfelt affection for many things in this world. But when the time comes for the eternal journey, they will have to abandon all these things and all of those who once were loved or relied upon in this world will have to be left behind being no longer be of any use. The things one loves most in this world are one's children and possessions. Lord Almighty explains in the following verses that even these cannot bring any benefit in the hereafter: *"The Day whereon neither wealth nor sons will avail, but only he (will prosper) that brings to Allah a sound heart"* (Shu'arà, 26: 88-89).

The Mathnawi: *"Whoever has a passion for that which is mortal does so only in the hope to reach the One that is truly alive and living. Thus, loving a mortal becomes a bridge to deep affection and takes one to Divine love."* (v.3: 545)

"O the one whose journey is to Allah! Exert yourself in the hope of the Living One, so that after some time the soul that you give does not become lifeless or get buried in the ground."

"Do not follow your desires and choose a piece of straw, i.e. a mortal beauty, as your friend. The affection and friendship in him are borrowed. Search for the permanent friend."

"If those to whom you gave your heart possessed any fidelity or constancy, then what has happened to your friendship with your mother and your father, who were your most faithful friends?" (v.3: 547-549)

"When the gold nature of that which you love turns to its original ugliness, when only the copper remains, your nature is surfeited and is separated from it." (v.3: 555)

"The beauty in mortals is only but a temporal reflection of Divine beauty. The reflecting light will return to its origin one day. O disciple, does not gaze on mortal or temporal beauty, but rather search for the One who gave them!"

"The light falling onto the wall from the sun returns to the sun. Do not look at the light on the wall, go to the one that sends the light, go to the sun; this is what you deserve."

"Henceforth take your water from heaven, as you have not found any faithfulness in the aqueduct." (v.3: 558-560)

The human disposition to affection is an invaluable treasure. It is a great loss for this love to be wasted in useless places. All friends in this world other than Allah who receive our love are absolute mortals. For this reason the main target of love and friendship should be the Lord Almighty. On the one hand, the Lord Almighty is beyond comprehension and distant from perception (*muta'âl*), but on the other, He is a friend and helper of His servant, He is closer than the jugular vein. If the servant arduously tries to get close to His Lord in his heart, then Allah Almighty announces that He will become *"His eyes with which he sees, his ears with which he hears, his hands with which he holds…"* (*Zubdat 'l-Bukhârî*, 1107). About this state it is said: «*For us Allah sufficeth, and He is the best disposer of affairs.*» (Âl 'Imrân, 3: 173)

When all is said, profane love, which is a heartfelt closeness and bonding with other than Allah, is only permissible when it is experienced as a temporary phase. In this case, that love becomes a phase on the path to Divine love. But, if that mortal being captivates the heart, it will become idolized and hinder Divine reunion. If one can become like Majnûn and say, "I found Mawlâ (my Lord) through Laylâ" and turn the profane love into a phase of reaching Divine love, what a blessing this is! "The love for Absolute Beauty" is the real love. To become its seeker is the greatest and noblest goal in this life.

The Mathnawi: *"I swear by the Holy Being of Allah, to Whom everything and everyone is in need but Who is not*

in need of anything or anyone, that a malignant snake is better than a malignant friend The malignant snake takes the life of a man. But a malignant friend leads him into the everlasting fire."

"The heart secretly steals the disposition from the disposition of the companion, without speech and talk his morals become yours."

"When he casts his shadow over you, that unprincipled friend steals away your capitals." (v.5: 2634-2637)

As we have stated before, "states are contagious", that is, being with a good person will produce a positive influence and being with a malignant person will produce a negative influence. The Prophet Muhammad (ﷺ) explained this with the following illustration: "The friendship of a good or a bad person is like the state of the perfume vendor and the blacksmith. The perfume vendor will either give you some perfume for free or you will buy it. You will (at least) have inhaled the beautiful scents (while you are with him). The blacksmit h will either burn your clothes or you will be uncomfortable with the disagreeable smell of his shop" (Bukhârî, *Dhabâ'ih*, 31).

Imam Rabbânî gave the following example of the perils that befalls one with corrupt friends.

"The person who is very close to gamblers might not be gambling. Thus, he will not feel tarnished. However, during the time he accompanies them he will start condoning gambling. And this is a spiritual disaster."

Consciously or not, abandoning such a shield, which is a necessary protection from any kind of sin, introduces the danger of falling into that sin at any moment. Companionship with crude or ignorant people will bring about a psychological proximity with them. In time, this proximity will turn into a heartfelt closeness and, little by little, one will be dragged into destruction.

The Mathnawi: *"The turpitude of befriending the hypocrites makes the believer wicked and rebellious like them."* (v.2: 2892)

The worst kind of wickedness is hypocrisy. The state of a hypocrite in Islam is worse than that of a "harmless heathen". A hypocrite's harm in misleading is far greater than that of a heathen who does not insinuate their ideas to people with blasphemy. For this reason, those who come to the greatest harm are those who befriend the hypocrites. Mental connection turns into a heartfelt relationship. This causes the ruin and disappointment of the believer. Mawlânâ indicated this reality in the previous verse.

The Mathnawi: *"Since in our eyes (foresight) there is much defect, go, let your own sight pass away in the sight of the friend."*

"His sight for ours - what a goodly recompense! In His sight you will find the whole object of your desire." (v.1: 921-922)

Although it may be bitter, friends always try to tell the truth. A friend will not shy away from telling the truth and will prefer to temporarily hurt a friend rather than see them endure a lasting harm. In some other verses, Mawlânâ Rûmî explains this with the story of a man who tells another man who has come to him for advice that he cannot help him.

"A man wanted advice on a matter for he could not arrive at a decision in order to get rid of his doubts. The person he wanted to consult said: "I appreciate the fact that you trusted me and came to me for advice. But I am not your friend. Go and find someone else and consult him. I am not your friend, so do not consult with me. One cannot succeed with the advice of one who is not a friend. Go and search for a friend. Surely a friend will want his friend's well being. I am not a friend; someone like me is of no use to you. I walk crookedly; I will tell you erroneous things. A man who befriends good people and spends time with them thinks he is in a rose garden, even if he is in a furnace. But the person sitting in a garden with the foe that he thinks is a friend will be sitting in a furnace. Come to your senses and do not belittle that genuine friend by giving into your ego, do not hurt him."

The Mathnawi: "*The heart takes nourishment from every friend. The heart receives spiritual joy, pleasure and purification from every piece of knowledge.*" (v.2: 1089)

"*You receive some spiritual nourishment from every person you meet. You also will receive something from every good friend.*" (v.2: 1091)

As we have mentioned above, we have to choose our friends very carefully. These verses of Mawlâna points to the benefits of befriending good people. Like we have said before, people's states are contagious. Love is the course through which the spiritual states transact. A human acquires the state of the person with whom they spend time in proportion to the affection felt for that person. Affection, according to its strength, will cause this relationship to increase. On the other hand, hate prevents this spiritual interaction between people, hence it should be turned towards the evil people.

The Mathnawi: "*Though you be a rock or marble, you will become a jewel when you reach a man who possesses a heart.*"

"Plant the love of the holy ones within your heart, do not give your heart to anything save to the love of them whose hearts know (Allah)."

"Do not go to the neighborhood of despair, there are gates of hope. Do not go in the direction of darkness, the suns are shining."

"The heart leads you into the neighborhood of the men who possess hearts; the body leads you into the prison of water and mud."

"Take heed! Give your heart nourishment from conversations with the one who is a friend of the heart." (v.1: 722-726)

The *nafs* guides humans in wretched directions. So, like an owner who tames a wild horse, we have to tame our *nafs* and make it righteous with knowledge and worship within the company of those who are on the path of Allah. Knowledge is essential for this, but it is not enough. People of knowledge should turn their knowledge into wisdom and reach maturity in their states and behaviour. Thus, the functions of heart and mind will move together in harmony. Otherwise, dry knowledge can drag a human into vanity, selfishness and destruction. The *nafs* has many degrees. A *nafs* that has never been trained is *ammâra*. Such a *nafs* will always desire wickedness, but with constant training it can be raised to the degrees of *lawwâma*, *mulhima* and *mutmai'nna*. When it reaches these stages, the fierce *nafs* has become like a tame horse and takes its owner to the Allah Almighty. True servanthood to Allah is seen at this stage. Only with the grace of Allah Almighty can one mature and reach the higher degrees of *radiyya*, *mardiyyah* and *kâmila*. One of the main conditions of reaching this state is togetherness and heartfelt affection with those who are close to Allah. An untamed *nafs* does not desire this. It will force you to be with worldly people. Yet, as there is ease with every hardship, there is ease with this too. It is enough that one should undertake this path. Reaching a stage higher than the angels can only be achieved through a trained *nafs*. When Adam was first created, the Divine imperative requiring the angels to prostrate to him was the result of this ability to take control of the *nafs*. The angels turn towards their Lord without any obstacles in their way, but for a human being, achieving this is only possible through rising above the obstacle of the *nafs*. The victory a human being achieves through spiritually reaching their Lord requires greater recognition and reward than that of the angels.

The Mathnawi: *"How can a friend turn aside from the pain inflicted by his friend? Pain is the kernel, and friendship is (only) as the husk. Has not joy in tribulation and calamity and suffering become the sign of (true) friendship? A friend is like gold, tribulation is like fire: gold becomes pure in the heart of the fire."* (v.2: 1459-1461)

There is an old saying: "A noble person is recognized in tribulations and a noble metal is recognized in fire." Indeed, in the same way that blessings are for us, remorse is also for us. However, there is a great danger of erring for those who object to either of these manifestations. In the face of ordeals, patience through the pursuit of genuine reasons results in Divine consent, while rebelling against ordeals can result in destruction. In a way, the blessings are the same. Knowing that a blessing is from Allah Almighty and being thankful to Him brings great prosperity and abundance, but to think that this blessing is from one's own power and to fall into arrogance and vanity will also result in destruction. Saints, those great souls, benefit from both blessings and ordeals and do not encounter harm due to these because they have strictly trained their understanding and perception in accord with revelation. So, they can say, "Your ordeals are as sweet as your blessings". With the grace of our Lord, we should strive to be like them. True benefit from ordeals and blessings does not stem from apparent causes that are self-evident, but rather from being content with the Real Cause behind all causes that is Allah Almighty (being content with whatever He gives) and comprehending the real reason, called *musabbibu'l asbâb* (the Causer of the causes). Those who achieve this, reach the state of *rizâ* (acceptance) and this is what Mawlânâ talks about in the verses mentioned above.

The Mathnawi: "*The wind of our maladies is strong and the candle of our life is almost out. Make haste; let us light another candle from the candle of our lives, so that we may continue our journey with one of the candles, if one of them be put out by the wind.*" (v.4: 3108-3109)

Mawlânâ conveys this truth in his verses and teaches us never to fall into despair. One should especially be aware of those states and actions that make one slip into wretchedness. The Lord Almighty has promised all His servants a chance to attain His mercy before their last breath, provided that there is true repentance.

Mathnawi: "*Oh, alas, alas for the sorrow and grief caused by a base friend! Oh sirs, seek you a good and a suitable companion!*" (v.6: 2950)

"*Take heed, do not become a worshipper of form and do not say this. Do not seek (to discover) the secret of congeniality in the outward form.*" (v.6: 2953)

Friendship is formed from mutuality be it in positive or negative attributes. But true friendship can only be harboured in sincere souls. This characteristic is found in the highest states of the human being. Friendship stays alive when both parties have the same emotions and share the same worldview. True friendship is a current between two hearts. With this current, with the flow of love, every state of the beloved radiates to the one who loves. The oceans of love in the soul start to rise and the suns of devotion start to burn. Therefore, the closeness felt by those who do not share mutual feelings and only have an external or coincidental affinity, for example, relations or casual friends, has no connection with true friendship. Thus, Abû Lahab was the Prophet's uncle, but he was amongst the unfortunate who were farthest from the Prophet.

The Truth of
Friendship

THE TRUTH OF FRIENDSHIP

*L*ove is like a stream which flows between two hearts. Those who love always remember their beloved with both their hearts and minds. They offer whatever they have to their beloved and having made these sacrifices, they live with peace of mind.

Friendship, in general, is about being together and sharing things, both good and bad. Real friendship, on the other hand, can only be found in the sincere souls of elevated personalities. Living friendship at its peak means that two people have the same feelings for all events; it is as if they have a unified heart that resides in two separate bodies.

A person adores and admires the person whom they love. Every state of the beloved is passed onto the lover because of a flow of love. The sea of love in the heart begins to swirl and the sun of ecstasy starts to shine. In the end, the lover relinquishes his own will and preferences and starts to imitate the beloved. In this sense a believer should know how to benefit from this elixir of love at every step in life.

True love turns burdens into blessings; likewise the sorrows that the beloved puts the lover through are welcomed as if they were favours. To understand the genuineness and depth of one's love, we need only to examine to what degree the lover can bear the sorrows of love. Mawlânâ Rûmî relates the following story that shows true love and friendship are only possible if both the sorrows and torment that come from the beloved are welcomed and only if the beloved is submitted to willingly.

A master received a melon as a gift from his visitors. He called upon Luqmân, the sensitive, perceptive servant, whom he loved dearly and with whom he was able to share his feelings. When Luqmân came, his master cut a slice of the melon and offered it to him. Luqmân ate that slice as if it was honey or sugar. He ate it with such delight and pleasure that the appetite of those who watched him was stimulated; in fact, they envied him. His master gave him another slice. Luqmân seemed to achieve peace and happiness through eating the melon. The master carried on giving him the melon until there was only one slice left. His master then said: "Let me eat this one and see how sweet it is."

The moment he bit the melon, the inside of his mouth burnt with its bitterness. His tongue was blistered and his throat became sore. He nearly fainted due to bad taste. He turned to Luqmân and said: "My dearest servant! How could you eat such poison with great delight? How could you take this difficulty as if it was a favour? What sort of patience is yours? Only Allah knows how much pain you have had to endure. Or are you an enemy of your own sweet life? Why did you not say anything? Why didn't you simply say «Excuse me but I cannot eat anything now»?

Luqmân replied: "I have eaten many delicious meals from your hand, dear master; you have nourished me both spiritually and physically with such rare things that I have to bow my head in embarrassment because I cannot return the gifts. How could

I possibly say «This is bitter, I can't eat it» for something you offered me with your hands? Moreover, however bitter, anything you offer is only sweet for me, because every particle in my body has been nourished by your blessings.»

Luqmân continued to share his excitement and love: "Dear master! If I resent a sorrow that comes from you, may my head be buried beneath the ground. How could a taste from your generous hand leave any trace of bitterness in this melon? Love makes sorrow sweet, love turns copper into gold. Love washes away the residue and purifies. Love heals unbearable pains. Love raises the dead. Love turns kings into subjects. Love makes rose gardens out of dungeons. Love illuminates dark rooms and makes them shine. It is because of love that fire becomes Divine light. Love brings beauty to the ugly. With love, sorrow and grief become happiness and joy. With love the bandits and seducers turn into guides to happiness. Because of love sickness turns into health and well-being. Love makes sorrow a blessing.»

Love is an instinct of the heart. However, the depth of love in the heart should be in accordance with the divinity of the Beloved. In this respect, Allah should be the ultimate recipient of this tendency of the heart to love. For the heart to attain the capability to experience the greatest love in every sense of the word, which is the love of Allah, it first needs to go through the levels of metaphorical love.

Forgetting the ultimate goal, which is to attain the love of Allah, by remaining at one of the temporary stations of love, such as the love for wealth, rank, commodities, family or children, means to drain the heart from one's world, and wasting that love. To overcome this obstacle one needs to remember that love of this kind is only «transient» and the value it deserves can only be to the extent of what it really is: a means to Divine love. In truth, this love comprises stations that must be experienced by the heart in order to be able to carry the love of Allah. Turning transient love into a step toward Divine love leads one to take a great delight in faith. A heedful person who is able to overcome worries and obsessions and contemplate the end of their life can easily see that they have been created for a purpose; therefore, it is necessary that a limit be put to worldly pleasures and transient loves, with our love being channelled towards a Divine goal.

Ridding one's temporary existence of egotistical desires and devoting it to the Divine Being takes one to immortality. Thus, life continues after the material body dies. The most typical example of this is Majnûn, who perfected the love he had for Laylâ in his heart, in the end attaining the love of the Lord. Had he not been able to transcend this love, Majnûn would only have been one of the millions of examples of transient love. His name would not have been worthy of being remembered for centuries, rather it would have been forgotten in history.

What is just and what is true can be known and understood not by reading but by the love that resides in the hearts. If the heart transcends through the stations of transient love to become immersed in the love of Allah, then all secrets, truths and beauties are manifested in it. Therefore, the true friendship that has the power to take one to felicity is 'friendship with the Lord'.

The following story of a conversation between a master and his slave is a good example which testifies to the truth of friendship with Allah:

A man bought a slave. The slave was a religious, praying believer who protected himself from what Allah forbade. When his master took the slave to his home, they had the following conversation: "What would you like to eat in my house?» the master asked.

The slave replied: «Whatever you give me.»

The master asked: «How would you like to be dressed?»

The slave replied: «Whatever you give me, I will wear it.»

The master asked: «In which room of my house would you like to stay?»

The slave replied: «In whichever room you want me to stay.»

The master asked: «What sort of work do you want to do in my house?»

The slave replied: «Whatever you want me to do, I will do it.»

After this last response, the master thought for a while and then spoke while trying to dry his tears: «I wish I was a friend like this to my Lord. That would be the greatest happiness.» Upon this, the slave said: «O my master! How could a slave have any other preference or will than his master's?» Then the master said: «I give you your freedom. You are free for Allah's sake. But I would like you to stay with me so I can serve you with my power and my money.»

Whoever knows Allah truthfully, and turns to Him with love, relinquishes their will and preferences to Him voluntarily; rather simply saying: «Why should I ask for anything from Allah?» A believer who loves their Lord needs to be aware of the fact that nothing really belongs to them, for they are to submit everything in their possession to their Beloved. This is because love requires sacrifice and there are no 'possessions' in its nature. Love brings a tendency to offer things both spiritual and material to the heart. This can be realized to the extent of the depth of one's love. For this reason, the greatest sacrifices are those that are made for love. One can even go so far for love as to give up one's life for the sake of the Beloved; the sacrifice depends on the depth of one's love. Allah Almighty confirms this fact in the following verse of the Qur'ân:

«*By no means shall you attain righteousness unless ye give (freely) of that which ye love....*" (Qur'ân, 3:92)

In this sense, the person who loves their Lord and remains faithful to the truth of this love submits to Him his self, his opportunities and his fate. It is not easy for a believer to claim to possess the love and friendship of Allah and His Messenger. The requirement for true love and friendship is to have no will but that of the Beloved. The state of the Prophet Ibrâhîm (upon him be peace) is exemplary as the pinnacle of being a friend of Allah.

When Nimrod was about to throw the Prophet Ibrâhîm into the fire, the angels came to help him. The Prophet Ibrâhîm said: "Who is the one that lights the fire? He is the one that knows every state of mine. I ask nothing from you. Do not come between two friends." As a result of his submission to Allah, the great fire into which Ibrâhîm was thrown turned into a rose garden.

Afterwards, Ibrâhîm (عليه السلام) prayed for a prophet to be among his descendants. Allah Almighty blessed him with a child in his old age and the Prophet Ibrâhîm loved this child very much. The innocent child conquered his heart. Yet in a dream he was instructed to sacrifice Ismâ'îl as a sign of this friendship and as part of his trial. However, the profound love that he had for his child made Ibrâhîm doubt the dream. It was only after the third time he had the same dream that Ibrâhîm was satisfied. He even threw stones at the Devil who tried to come between him and his Lord by introducing doubts and misgivings.

Ibrâhîm was willing to sacrifice his transient love for the sake of his love of the Friend Who is Eternal, Allah. And after seeing his determination, and as a sign of friendship, his Eternal Friend returned his son to him and sent him a ram to sacrifice. Allah says in the Qur'ân:

«We called out to him, 'O Ibrâhîm! Thou hast already fulfilled the vision!' – thus indeed do We reward those who do right; for this was obviously a trial – and we ransomed him with a momentous sacrifice. And We left (this blessing) for him among generations (to come) in later times: "Peace and salutation to Ibrâhîm!" (Qur'ân, 37: 104-109)

And with this, the Prophet Ibrâhîm's friendship with Allah was announced to humanity.

Those who become friends with Allah are also friends with what He has created. They acquire the capability to see things through the lens of the Lord. Our master, our Prophet, the Honour of the Worlds, who is at the pinnacle of friendship with Allah, prayed to His Lord for the people of Ta'if while they were throwing stones at him, asking for them to be brought to the straight path rather than be destroyed.

Hallâj al-Mansûr, another friend of Allah who went through one of the toughest trials of friendship, was so overcome by manifestations of miracles that in the end he could not contain his ecstasy and revealed secrets that were meant to be private. While those who were unaware of the spiritual state he was in were throwing stones at him, he was praying to Allah: "Dear Lord! Forgive those who are throwing stones at me even before

I forgive them, for they do not know what I am experiencing. It is only because of my religious zeal that they are attacking me." This prayer is an example of the true nature of compassion and forgiveness towards people. It also brings to us an exemplary moment of looking at the creation through the lens of our Lord.

It is only after one overcomes the obstacle of the egotistical self that one is able to gain the strength to be patient in the face of trials and difficulties for the sake of Allah. After all, it is Allah who has lovingly sent them our way. Such situations are only natural in the spiritual path. The biggest rewards and the greatest friendships are earned only after the display of tremendous persistence, patience, determination and endurance.

In the eyes of believers who attain this level, happiness and sorrow are the same; this is because their hearts are no longer attached to the world, and therefore pain and pleasure are all equal. They know that whatever happens, be it good or bad, is a result of Divine providence and they are content with it. The following lines express this beautifully:

Whatever comes from You (Oh Allah) is pleasant to me;

Be it rosebuds or thorns!

A shroud or a robe of honour;

I enjoy both your wrath and your favour!

To apply the sentiment of this quatrain to life takes great courage and endurance; it is not easy to do. One needs to be careful not to utter words like these prematurely and heedlessly out of self-pride or in imitation, for these words can only be said at the level of *radiyyah* (the pleased self). Otherwise, if Allah Almighty were to put His servant through a trial to test the genuineness of such a claim, it is feared that the servant may fail.

In short, the felicity of the heart lies in being happy with what Allah has sent our way. Nothing else can yield any true benefit. Mawlânâ Rûmî says it most beautifully:

"So long as you are not happy with what Allah has given you, you will find tragedy waiting for you wherever you search for comfort or salvation; disaster will come and you will be stricken. May you know that there is not a single corner of this world that is free of calamities. Only by finding Allah in your heart, by seeking refuge in Him and by living in His presence can you attain comfort and salvation. Look at those who live in the safest places in this world and who are deemed to be the most powerful; do they not fall prey to death in the end too? Seek refuge in Allah instead of trying to keep yourself safe from these transient pitfalls! If He so wishes, He can turn poison into an antidote for you and if He so wishes He can make water poison for you!"

Dear Lord! Enable us helpless servants to benefit from the world of the heart of Your friends in the best possible way. Allow us to have a share of the manifestation of this noble verse from the Qur'ân: *"Behold! Verily on the friends of God there is no fear, nor shall they grieve."* (Qur'ân, 10:62) Âmîn!

Eternal Love and Muhammedan Light in the Mathnawi

ETERNAL LOVE AND MUHAMMEDAN LIGHT IN THE MATHNAWI

*T*he **Mathnawi:** *"O heart! True happiness is reaching the Prophet Muhammad (May God bless him and grant him peace)). The radiance of the universe is from the light of his blessed beauty."* (v.6; 1861)

In pre-eternity (*azal*) there existed only the Lord Almighty; He wanted to be known by man and jinn (*marifatullah*) through their elevation of themselves in worship; He thus created this universe. The first to be formed in this creation was the light (*nûr*) of Muhammad. On this matter the Prophet Muhammad (صلى الله عليه وسلم) said:

"I was a messenger when Adam was between soul and body." (Tirmidhî, *Manâqib*, 1). Although the actual essence of our Prophet (صلى الله عليه وسلم) -the "Nûr of Muhammad"- was the first creation, his was the last delegation as a mercy to all humanity within a body known by the title of Prophet. The calendar of Prophethood started with the first creation, the "Nûr of Muhammad" and was completed with the last stage, which was the "physical existence of Muhammad".

The "Nûr of Muhammad" is the essence and initiator of the Truth of Muhammad. Before the "Nûr of Muhammad", which is like a precious jewel protected in an elegant case without being revealed to the entire creation, everything else was created for his sake. The primary reason for creation is the Lord Almighty's Own existence, while the secondary reason is the need to envelope and ornament the "Nûr of Muhammad" with the rest of creation. Indeed, in another *hadîth* the Prophet says:

"When the Prophet Adam realized his fault that caused him to be expelled from heaven he said, "O Lord! I ask for your forgiveness for the sake of Muhammad (ﷺ)." The Lord Almighty asked him, "O Adam! How do you know about Muhammad although I have not yet created him?" Adam replied, "O Lord! When you created me and breathed into me from Your soul I raised my head and saw the words *lâ ilâha illallâh Muhammadun Rasûlallâh* on the pillars of the highest heaven. I understood that you would only join that which is the most beautiful of creation to your own name." After this Allah Almighty said "You have spoken the truth O Adam! To Me, he is the most delightful of all creation. Pray to Me for his sake. (And since you have) I forgive you. If, perchance, Muhammad (ﷺ) did not exist, I would not have created you." (Hâkim, *Mustadrak*, II: 672; Bayhaqî, *Dalâ'il*, V: 488-489)

The manifestation of love within a human being is the first sign of the presence of a heart. The perfection of this state is to feel love towards the most deserving, namely Allah Almighty and His beloved Prophet.

The Mathnawi: *"Know, o son, that everything in the universe is like a jug filled to the brim with wisdom and beauty. But this beauty and knowledge is a drop from the Tigris, which belongs to Allah, the appearance of whom is*

71

necessitated by His existence, and it is not possible for Him not to appear. He was a hidden treasure, which, because of its fullness surged up and made the earth, which He made brighter than the sky, (like) a sultan robed in satin. (v.1: 2860-2863)

Allah Almighty is not confined by time or location. He is present in a state that is without time or space and only He knows His own truth. The Lord Almighty's existence is absolute but the existence of the rest of creation is contingent.

Therefore, the Lord Almighty, who exists in eternity and who does not need another creator for His existence, wished to be known intellectually by both humans and the jinn and wished to be glorified with the worship that would be the outcome of the conscience that is necessitated by this knowledge, and thus he created this universe, known as "the universe of multitude".

This truth is made known through the Hadith Qudsî[14] that starts *"I was a secret treasure…"* (Ismâ'îl Haqqî Bursawî, *Kanz-i Makhfî*). This *hadîth* is a basic code of law for the lives of all humanity helping them to understand the reason for the creation of the universe we live in so that we can turn towards achieving that wisdom.

The Mathnawi: *"Know that the one whose heart is without Divine love or passion is wretched. The dog of the Companions of the Cave searched for the souls of love, and thus found them and reached a spiritual stage and those servants attained the heavens."* (v.2: 1425; 1428)

The People of the Cave (*Ashâb al-Kahf*) were a small group of young people who are mentioned in the Qur'ân as faithful

---

14.   Revelations of Allah Almighty that were not a part of the Qur'ân but transmitted to us in the sayings of the prophet (pbuh).

believers in the Oneness of God. These young people strove to live according to their belief and did not hesitate to declare their faith, trying to avoid the blasphemy, corruption and oppression that were practiced by the society in which they lived. They had to leave the city and take refuge in a cave since their lives were in danger. On their way to the cave, a dog, Kitmir, joined them and became their watchdog. King Dakyânus and his soldiers followed these young people and when they came to the mouth of the cave, instead of killing the young people, the soldiers sealed up the entrance and left them to die. Three hundred years passed and as a mercy from their Lord these young people slept throughout this time until they awoke.

Contemplating on the Qur'ânic verses about these people (Kahf, 18: 9-22) Rûmî indicates the state of Kitmir and says that being together with those who are true believers and people of love can elevate even a dog to a state of "those who are from heaven". He urges us to think of the blessings a human may receive if he were to be in the place of Kitmir, reminding us of the blessings, beyond our imagination, that were showered on a dog for being together with these people. He encourages us to be on this path, pointing to the abundance of joining the pious and the faithful. This also is a Qur'ânic teaching as the Lord Almighty says: "...be with those who are true (in word and deed)" (Tawba, 9: 119)

The beloved Prophet has informed us that there are no animals in heaven except Kitmir and a few other animals who gained admittance there due to some distinguished qualities.

The Mathnawi: *"By love dregs become clear; by love a dead heart is made living and the king is made a slave"* (v.2: 1530-1531)

Rûmî uses the phrase *"By love dregs become clear"* to show the prosperous results of love and affection in a human's life.

Truly, when there is love, pain is transformed into mercy and hardship becomes ease. When one embarks on a road with love, they will find ability, merit and perception when faced with hardships. Even in one's personal and daily life, if they love what they are doing, the hardships that are faced either disappear or lessen and to become insignificant in proportion with this love. The Companions traveled to far places like Constantinople, Samarkand and China to convey the message of Islam because of their commitment to it and their love for Lord Almighty and His Prophet. These travels were difficult, harsh and dangerous but they did not tire. Their love for their faith and the traces of light of the Prophethood they carried within their hearts turned the suffering of these long and difficult journeys into pleasure. Due to his worldly and metaphorical love, dig through a mountain was easy for Farhâd[15] and he overcame this difficult task with pleasure.

Love is as strong as the merit of the being it is directed towards. For this reason, the most exalted and bountiful love is the love of Allah; this is the love and passion felt by the servant towards their Lord. There is no other being that can be worthy of such a great love except Him. He is the creator of love. In a verse where the love of the believers for Allah is described it is said:

---

15. Farhâd and Shirîn is a story of Persian origin which is found in the great epico-historical poems of Shahnameh; it was based on a true story which was further romanticized by Persian poets. The story depicts the love of Sassanian Khusraw Parviz for a Christian princess, Shirîn. Khusraw o Shirin recounts the story of King Khusraw's courtship of Princess Shirin, and how he vanquished his rival, Farhâd, by sending him into exile to Mt. Behistun with the impossible task of carving stairs out of the cliff rocks.

"...But those of Faith are overflowing in their love for Allah..." (Baqarah, 2: 165)

Humans pay the highest price for their love. It was easy for Farhâd to dig through the mountains for Shirîn and it was also easy for Majnûn[16] to live in the desert for the sake of Laylâ. If one thinks that figurative love drives people to such great selflessness that they abandon their lives for their love, it seems insignificant for one to sacrifice a thousand lives for Divine love. The lovers wish to sacrifice from their identities and even their own life in proportion to the love they feel. For this reason the Companions of the Prophet lived a life in which they sacrificed their lives and goods for Allah Almighty and His Prophet with a sense of gratitude. Their response to the smallest wish of the Prophet would often be "My mother and father be sacrificed for you and my life and my goods, O Messenger of Allah!"

The soldiers of Fâtih Sultân Mehmet were struggling to be one of those mentioned in the following *hadîth*, "Certainly, Constantinople will be conquered. What a blessed commander and what a blessed army!" (Ahmad, IV, 335; Hâkim, IV, 468:8300) They would be heard saying "today it is our turn to become martyrs" with an exuberant belief and enthusiasm as they were climbing the ramparts of Byzantium with hot oil and fire being poured down onto them.

As we ponder the sacrifices mentioned above that are made for human love, we should consider how reaching the peak of this inclination of love could affect a believer, a lover of Truth, if it is aimed at Allah Almighty and His Messenger.

---

16.   Another similar love story where Majnun goes mad after he is separated from his beloved Laylâ

In spirituality, the affections that flourish from Divine springs are like the flowers of the gardens of heaven; the breeze brings us thousands of scents. Even if at times the leaves fall off or the flowers wilt, the plant will still find nourishment, happiness and blessings with the light of spring.

But those affections that cannot find the place they deserve are sad wastes of this mortal life. The affections that are in the claws of worthless and lowly interests are like flowers on the pavement, which are bound to be trampled and ruined. What a shame if a diamond falls into the street. What a catastrophe to be afflicted with an incompetent heart.

The Mathnawi: *"It is not possible to reach Divine love and affection without burning the body"* (v.1: 22)

As we have mentioned in the explanation of the verse, when the servant turns towards his Creator with deep affection and turns this affection into real love then the mortal being and all the possibilities relating to that person will fall out of sight and lose their importance. "Me" and "you" will disappear. Selfishness will leave and the mortal being will be revived with the "You" pointing to Allah.

To restate this fact, unless we save our heart from the world, its blessings and the love of these, the lightning of Divine love will never shine on our world and Divine blessings will not be unveiled. Love of Allah cannot be realized until the heart has been cleansed from the love of the world.

Mawlânâ says:

"Do not be like the raindrop that is frightened of the wind and the dirt. Both of these will destroy the raindrop; the wind will dry it out and the dirt will absorb it. But if that raindrop could leap to the sea it will be saved from the heat

of the sun and the wind and dirt. The visible being of that raindrop will vanish into the sea but its self and its truth will always remain as a particle of that sea.

When a mortal being surrenders to an eternal being it becomes eternal and immortal. O you who are like a raindrop compared to this universe. Before you regret it come to your senses and give your being to Allah in order to reach true happiness. Give it so that in return for your life, which is like a raindrop, you will reach the sea and become the endless sea itself. Pull yourself together and sacrifice your life to this excellence; go into the palms of the sea and be saved from perishing in the labyrinths of the nafs!"

The Mathnawi: *"Matters of love, affection and friendship are bound to loyalty and they always search for those who are loyal. They never approach a disloyal heart."* (v.5: 1165)

Loyalty in a human being is a result of stability. Nothing can be reached with affections that flare up or fade like the maybug. The one who is stable in their soul is a human who, once they have learnt about the pleasures of Divine love, will not return but continue on this way until they forgo their mortal self. The hearts of those without such stability cannot bear Divine love for long. This means that these people are unable to comprehend the blessings they have. However, if the comprehension is absolute, then the pleasure that is tasted will be a continuing attribute of that person until the time of their death.

Love and affection cannot harbor in a heart where there is no stability, and as a result, no loyalty. Consequently, if it does not find this attribute, the love of Allah -due to its intensity- will not transcend into that heart. Loyalty and self-sacrifice are the most important measures that indicate the level of the heart.

Avoiding self-sacrifice and deprivation of loyalty are a betrayal of love and friendship.

The Mathnawi: *"The river will stop being a river when it reaches the sea; it will become a part of the sea."* (v.4: 2619)

"A piece of bread we eat disappears into our body and becomes a part of our body. (The existence of a person who is in love will disappear within the lover in proportion to the strength of the love that is felt)." (v.1: 3166)

"If there had not been love, how could there have been existence? How would bread give itself to you and become a part of your body and become you?

"The bread gave itself to you and became you. Why? From love and want! Otherwise, would it have given way to become life in your body?"

"Love even gives life to lifeless bread, adds its mortal life to you and makes it immortal!" (v.5: 2012-2014)

Affection makes the lover and the loved one become alike, otherwise, one of them will disappear within the other.

As the affection increases, it starts to absorb everything about the being that it has turned towards and penetrates into the world of his/her beloved. For example, when a person has a very strong love for another, he feels various levels of affection for the city where his beloved was born or the people of that city or people who resemble the loved one or those who carry the same name. This is also called the "conscious depth" of love. Muhammad Iqbal, the famous Pakistani thinker, loved Mawlânâ Jalâluddîn Rûmî to such an extent that when his plane entered the Turkish air zone he involuntarily stood up and shouted "Now we have entered the homeland of Mawlânâ".

The reason why Medina holds a throne in people's hearts as *Madinat l-Nabî* is the fact that it sheltered the last Prophet. When the Prophet (ﷺ) or his city of Medina are mentioned a sweet breeze is felt in the hearts. Again, the reason why 'Uhud is so cherished and distinguished amongst thousands of other mountains is the fact that the Prophet (ﷺ) himself had a special attachment towards it.

When such love expands and subsumes all the creation within it, it is called "absolute love". The only being that all other beings can attach themselves to is the Lord Almighty, because everything has come into existence with a glimmer of His attribute of Creator. This means that true love is only possible by steering the affection towards Allah Almighty to the extent that all existence will be surrounded by it because of their connection to Him. Gazing through His sight will begin at this point. The snake will cease to be terrifying. When looked at from this point of view absolute love is an action that belongs only to Allah.

We ascribe some other attributes of Allah to other beings, particularly to human beings. For example, we call someone **'âlim** (knowledgeable) or **'âdil** (just), but we do not mean that those humans are all knowing like Allah. If we did so this would be *shirk*.[17] When using these adjectives for those other than Allah we must not forget the Divine attribute that describes Allah as *Mukhalif li'l-hawâdith*, meaning, he is absolutely dissimilar to anything that has been created. By using the title *'âlim* or *'âdil* we express that a person has received a share from these Divine attributes according to their human potential and capacity. Love is also exactly like this and for this reason, in reality, the only "love" and the only "lover" is Allah Himself.

---

17.   Assigning partners to Allah.

A mortal human being can be called a "lover" to the degree of their share that is a manifestation of mercy and benefaction in a universe Allah has surrounded with mercy, compassion and love. Those who reach this degree are in a state called *fanâ fillâh*, they are the ones who annihilate themselves in Allah, purify themselves from all claims and reach the peak and joy of transience. The moment the raindrop tastes the ocean it means that it has received its share and has reached it.

There is a lovely expression:

*"When you lose yourself
Only the Lord remains."*

The Mathnawi: *"Whether love is from the self or from the spirit, in the end it is a guide that leads us yonder."* (v.1: 111)

"Choose the love of Allah who is everlasting so that He will give you the wine of true meaning and give you life" (v.1: 219)

"Choose the love of He from Whose love all the Prophets gained power and glory, honor and felicity." (v. 1: 220)

All forms of legitimate love are esteemed as they guide humans in reaching glory, as these forms of love attune the person to self-sacrifice and relief from the will of the *nafs*.

Spouses, offspring and property are steps that help reach high goals and are rehearsals that help attain Divine unity when they are loved for Allah within the boundaries that are assigned by Him. But making this love, granted by the Lord, into a toy and exaggerating it to a state of an idol is not acceptable. If one lets the sea water into the ship, that needs to be under it, this means the destruction and sinking of the ship.

For a believer, loving anything other than Allah with an affection that is as strong as "true love" is not acceptable. These transient affections are pardoned only when they are a station on the way to Divine love. If the servant of Allah loves another creature other than Allah with a great affection, and if this affection subsequently takes root in the heart, then this is *shirk*. In a verse of the Qur'ân we read:

"*Seest thou such a one as taketh for his god his own passion (or impulse)?*" (Furqân, 25: 43, also Jâthiya, 45: 23)

Among these transient affections and strong attachments that are provided to prepare the grounds for Divine love and to increase the aptitude for loving Allah, affection towards goods and offspring is the most dangerous; in the Qur'ân we read: "*And know ye that your possessions and your progeny are but a trial...*" (Anfâl, 8: 28). This danger of sedition becomes clear when the strength and the constancy of the affection felt for children and goods is contemplated; however, loving the creation is permissible within the lawful boundaries as a transitory station. It is condoned and allowed as a training ground for the heart: it helps us to prepare for Divine love.

The Mathnawi: "*Oh, the life of lovers consists in death: thou will not win the (Beloved's) heart except in losing your own.*" (v.1: 1751)

As we have mentioned before, the lover is inclined to be lost in the beloved, and they cherish this. The Companions of the Prophet used all their means and were ready to sacrifice themselves. Whenever they could they would respond as follows: "I sacrifice my life and possessions for you, O Messenger of Allah!" The actualization of this state is the ultimate satisfaction of the yearning for the love of Allah. The moths that were able to receive a minute share of this condition were called *pervane*; they threw themselves in the fire to prove their love. Muhammad Iqbal writes about this in a poem:

"One night I heard a clothes moth talking to a pervane:

"I dwelled in the books of Avicenna. I saw the books of Al-Farabi. (I wandered through the endless dry lines and among the faded letters and ate them away. I roamed every street and road of al-Madinatu'l Fadila of Farabi, which means the city of the graceful but) I could not possibly understand the philosophy of this life. I became a sad traveler of dead end roads full of nightmares. I have no sun to shine on my days."

The *pervane* displayed its charred wings to the clothes moth after hearing this and said:

"Look! I have burnt my wings for this love," and continued, "What makes life more full of life are the struggles of love; love gives wings to life!"

What the *pervane* was trying to say to the clothes moth was,

"Save yourself from perishing on these benighted, steep roads of philosophy. Open your wings to unity by taking a share from the ocean of spirituality that are full of love, fascination and prosperity."

Love begins with struggle. Reaching unity by transcending the ocean of life becomes true on the abundant and fertile grounds of love and fascination.

Eternal Affection and the Muhammedan Light

ETERNAL AFFECTION AND THE MUHAMMEDAN LIGHT

$\mathcal{T}$he following is a famous *hadîth qudsî*, or saying of Allah:

"I was a hidden treasure, and I wished to be known; this is why I created the universe."

Thus we can understand that the universe and the whole of creation consist of Divine love. This is the reason why people see the world with a deep stirring in the soul, perceiving all the worldly belongings and wealth as a sign of love and affection, and why they realize that Allah Almighty has created everything; they accept this as evidence of His abilities and perfection. Mawlânâ Rûmî explains the importance of love and affection for humans in the following lines:

"Know how pitiful is he who does not possess divine love and affection; he may even be inferior to a dog, because the dog of the Companions of the Cave [18] searched for tamed love, and

---

18. The Companions of the Cave were a group of young people who, fleeing oppression, entered a cave and were made by Allah to fall asleep and reawaken 100 years later. The dog mentioned here was guarding the door of the cave to keep the group safe and due to his proximity to the group, was also a recipient of the blessings of this Divine miracle.

found it; he reached spiritual pleasure and those special mortals attained heaven."

The pious know that the reason for their creation is the bud of eternal affection, the Prophet Muhammad (ﷺ): 'O beloved! If it was not for you I would not have created the universe.' Complimented with the title 'The Light of Creation', the Prophet Muhammad (May God bless him and grant him peace), has had the universe dedicated to him.

The First and Last Page of the Calendar of Prophethood

The Prophet Muhammad (ﷺ), whose Divine light appeared before Adam, but who physically appeared after all the other Messengers, was both the first and the last in the line of Prophets. In respect of creation, the Prophet Muhammad (ﷺ) was the first, but in respect of time, he was the last Prophet. As he was the reason for the entire creation, Allah Almighty blessed him with the title **'Beloved'.** The Prophet Muhammad's exceptional life was established by Allah Almighty in the most beautiful way, both spiritually and physically, and he was then blessed as a Mercy for the whole of mankind.

The manners and personality of the Prophet Muhammad (ﷺ) and his behaviour towards mankind are an example for all. Allah Almighty created the Prophet Muhammad as an example of perfect character for everyone. This is why he was sent into the community as a pitiful orphan, passing through all the grades and levels of society and stages of life, becoming a head of state and Prophet; thus he reached the highest rank of authority and power. His display of excellent behaviour and actions, his intelligence, and his capabilities and power are an example for human beings at any level or rank. In fact, the Prophet Muhammad (ﷺ) was sent by Allah the Merciful as an example for all of mankind from the time he was appointed to the Prophethood until the Day of Judgment. We are told in the following verse:

"Ye have indeed in the Messenger of Allah an excellent exemplar for him who hopes in Allah and the Final Day, and who remembers Allah much." (Ahzâb, 33: 21)

We can understand from this that it is our duty to study the life and actions of the Prophet Muhammad (ﷺ) in order to attain this excellent temperament, faith and spiritual intuition. Every human must wrap themselves in his spirituality and affection in order to be able to apply their own knowledge and instincts when following his blessed example.

Before becoming a prophet, Muhammad lived a contented and dignified life, believing in the unity of Allah. In particular, during the period immediately before he was blessed with the duty of Prophethood, he would spend much of his time in worship, retreating to the Mountain of Light (Hirâ) and absorbing himself in deep contemplation.. The reason for this seclusion was the blatant perversity of his society and the sadness and affection he felt for those who were oppressed or destitute. In reality, all these trials were but a preparation by Allah Almighty to reveal the Qur'ân to mankind via the Prophet. The Qur'ân was to be our guide for life and it was to come to us through the holy heart of the Messenger. In the following Qur'ânic verse we learn:

"Say: Whoever is an enemy to Gabriel - for he brings down the (revelation) to thy heart by Allah's will, a confirmation of what went before, and guidance and glad tidings for those who believe." (Baqarah, 2: 97)

With these experiences, the Prophet Muhammad's heart had reached a state of purity and a level from which he could comment upon and instruct in the revelations. The Prophet's heart had now been prepared for the Revelation; for six continuous months he had received spiritual signs and inspirations. For an average person to take up such a heavy burden would have been impossible; normal human beings are not created with this kind of capability. But for the Prophet Muhammad (ﷺ), the mysterious veil of spirituality had been removed and it was time for this gift and power of mystery to surface.

This Honoured One of the Universe had combined the duties and power of all the Prophets with his actions and character. In the Prophet Muhammad (ﷺ) nobility and dignity, moral quality and the manifestation of Divine perfection reached their peak. Commandments were given. Instruction was provided for 'cleansing of the heart' and 'purification of the *nafs*', and with a pure heart he taught the prayers and servant-hood which were to be performed in front of Allah Almighty. By living and displaying the best of morals, the

Muhammad became the most perfect example of humanity.

The Essence of *Tasawwuf* (Islamic Spirituality)

The essence of *tasawwuf* is to attain a pure and healthy soul that has dedicated itself to the love for Allah; these are the cause of the Divine union of the soul. The spiritual events that happened to Prophet Muhammad (ﷺ) prior to receiving the Revelation, the purification of his soul and the cleansing of his ego are all a part of the grounds for *tasawwuf*.

Certainly, the Prophet Muhammad's heart and soul had attained a high spiritual level before he received the Revelation; the holy Prophet lived a life of good conduct and divinity.

However, when he returned from the Mountain of Light, Hirâ, with the Divine order, it was obvious that he had reached a glorious phase that was very different from his former life.

Spiritually communicating with Allah Almighty, absorbing every speck of light from the glory of unification and the merits of Allah, the Prophet Muhammad (ﷺ) had reached the peak of faith and submission; he would stand in prayer until his feet were swollen, shedding tears in adoration while still continuing his Divine service. Even when he slept, the Prophet Muhammad's heart was always alert; he never distanced himself from Allah's remembrance or contemplation for a single moment.

With the blessing of Allah, the Prophet Muhammad (ﷺ) attained this nature of his heart and a state of perfection; he continued to convey the message of Islam to all of mankind, aware of the Divine trust that he had been endowed with and which lifted him to the peak of all peaks. Prophet Muhammad rejected anything that would reflect on or prevent him from carrying out the Divine duty that had been bestowed upon him and he acknowledged the duty of worshipping Allah Almighty over everything else.

It is essential to begin first with praising the Lord of the Universe, the result of which is the purification of the heart from evil feelings, thoughts, and preoccupations; only then can the Qur'ân, which orders that the whole of creation take refuge in Allah alone, be a book of guidance for mankind until the Day of Judgment. The Prophet Muhammad (ﷺ) and his lifetime of actions are the guide for human conduct. Affection for the Prophet Muhammad is affection for Allah, obedience to him is obedience to Allah and rebellion against him is rebellion against Allah. Thus the blessed existence of the Prophet Muhammad is a refuge of affection for mankind.

89

Tasawwuf is the unification of that which is evident and that which is hidden in the life of the Prophet Muhammad (ﷺ) and is a blend of great affection. This is because every act of the Prophet Muhammad is a form of the essence of *tasawwuf* in that every action aims to make the heart pure, the ego (*nafs*) clean, and the soul healthy so that the human is prepared for his "Divine union" with his creator in the most excellent way.

In another account, it is stated that *tasawwuf* is a Divine privilege, starting with the 'blowing of the soul' into Adam (عليه السلام) and ending with the vision of the perfection, His Messenger, on the Day of Judgment. It is the reflection of the dew of prosperity on hearts full of affection.

Prophetic Morality in the Mathnawi

PROPHETIC MORALITY IN THE MATHNAWI

The Mathnawi: *"I am in love with the One to Whom everything belongs; everything is His creation. My intellect and my life are given as a sacrifice to His beloved."* (v.3: 4136)

'Ashq is the name given to the ultimate power and capability of love. Ultimate love is intended for Allah Almighty and it is only when one loves Him that they can reach perfection in 'ashq. The way to achieve this is through transcending the phases of earthly love, known as figurative 'ashq. The most abundant love in this aspect is the love of the Messenger of Allah (ﷺ); he was a gift to the universe from the Creator of all things.

In the verses above Rûmî declares that by sacrificing his intellect and life to the Prophet - who was *Habîbullah* (beloved of Allah) - he has been able to reach *mahabbatullah*, the love of Allah. The Companions of the Prophet are the best examples of this. Their reply to the slightest wish of the Prophet was "May all my life and wealth be sacrificed for you; say what you desire, O, Messenger of Allah!"

The Mathnawi: *"Each of you is a sheep; the Prophet is the shepherd. The people are like the flock and he is the overseer.*

The shepherd is not afraid of the sheep in (his) contention (with them), but is their protector from heat and cold.

If he cries out in wrath against the flock, realize that this is because of the love he has for them all." (v.3: 4146-4148)

Referring to human beings as a flock of sheep in the above verses is not meant to be degrading. It is to draw attention to our state, that is we either rule like a shepherd or being ruled like the sheep. Indeed in a *hadîth*, the Prophet says, *"You are all shepherds and you are responsible from those who you shepherd."* (Bukhârî, Jumu'a 11, Istikrâz 20; Muslim, 'Imâra 20). This shows us that ever human being has the capacity to rule others; with this power comes a certain responsibility. Shepherds are often seen carrying a sick animal that has been left behind in order to reunite it with the flock. The most distinguished attributes of a shepherd are mercy, compassion, sincerity; one who directs others should always hold the people for whom they are responsible close to their heart.

The Mathnawi: *"The Qur'ân is the explanation of the qualities of the Prophets. If you read and practice it, then consider yourself as having visited the Prophets and saints.*

If you do not abide by the rules and live according to the morals of the Qur'ân even though you have read it, what benefit will come to you of seeing the Prophets and the saints?

As one reads the stories of the Prophets thoroughly, this bodily cage will become narrow for the bird of soul." (v.1: 1516-1518)

The Qur'ân has been sent to people as a guidance (*hidâya*): it shows the way to reach happiness in this world and in the Hereafter. In order to achieve this, the Qur'ân guides us by touching upon different subjects in various styles and with different declarations. Among these subjects, the stories about the Prophets and their peoples hold a particularly important place. Those who read the Qur'ân gain a great deal of information about the blessings that were given to the Prophets and the pious whom Allah is pleased with, as well as about the destruction of the heathens and oppressors who rebel against the Almighty; with this knowledge they will be able to organize their lives as the people of steadfastness (istiqâmah).

In order to receive the utmost benefit from the stories of the Prophets mentioned in the Qur'ân, a person should also prepare their inner world. Indeed, Allah says in the Qur'ân that failure to contemplate the profound meanings of the verses is due to a seal on the hearts.

"Will they not, then, ponder over this Qur'ân? - or are there seals upon their hearts?" (Muhammad, 47: 24)

According to this verse, to understand, comprehend, feel and grasp the secrets of the Qur'ân one must have a sound heart, as the Qur'ân will open its secrets only to a sound heart. The Messenger of Allah (ﷺ) was the greatest commentator of the Qur'ân so, in essence, all of his traditions (hadîth) are an explanation of it. After the Prophet, the greatest and the most accurate interpreters are those scholarly saints who practice what they know and who have a share in the spiritual life of the Prophet. On this subject Mawlânâ says:

"Those who understand the Qur'ân are those who practise it."

A heart that is blackened with fleshly desire have nothing to take from the Qur'ân. Western orientalists who study Islam have outward knowledge, but because they do not live a spiritual life, the Qur'ân does not open its secrets to them and it does not show them guidance. Allah Almighty says:

"...for, though they may see every sign [of the truth], they do not believe in it, and though they may see the path of rectitude, they do not choose to follow it-whereas, if they see a path of error, they take it for their own: this, because they have given the lie to Our messages, and have remained heedless of them." (A'râf, 7: 146)

The purpose of reading the Qur'ân is to be adorned with its manners. When asked about the morals of the Prophet (ﷺ) after he had passed away, his wife 'Â'isha (r.a.) said:

"His manners were the Qur'ân" (Muslim, *Musâfirîn* 139; Nasâ'î, *Qiyâmu'l layl*, 2)

The Qur'ân comprises rules and regulations that have been sent to bring a morality to mankind that is higher than that of the angels. In the aforementioned verses, Rumi conveys the message that reading the Qur'ân and understanding it will enable a person to adorn himself with the morals of the beloved Prophet. The Prophet has presented this as *Divine morality* and he ordered his *Ummah* to be *assume the character traits of the Lord Almighty.* (Munâwî, *al-Ta'ârif*, p. 564)

The story of Ibn 'Abbâs (ﷺ) is a good example of Qur'ânic morality. Once, a man said some unpleasant things to Ibn 'Abbâs (ﷺ), but the latter merely remained quiet. The man was astounded and asked Ibn 'Abbâs why he did not retaliate. To this, Ibn 'Abbâs responded:

"There are three traits I assume which stop me from retaliating against you: firstly, when I read a verse from the book of Allah, I wish for every man to know what I have *been graced to read; secondly, I become very happy when I*

hear that a Muslim judge has served justice, though I have no familial ties with that judge; thirdly, I become very happy when rain falls on land owned by Muslims though I have no animals grazing on that particular land nor own any land there myself."[19] (Haythamî, *Majmû al-Zawâ'id*, v. 9, pg. 284)

The Mathnawi: *"There are melodies within Prophets which revive; these melodies bestow a priceless life on those who are in search of the Truth."* (v.1: 1919)

A life can only be meaningful and valuable through accurate ideas and behavior. This means reaching to the truth and the good. The most exceptional and unique guides in doing this are the Prophets, because Allah Almighty made all of them, especially the Prophet Muhammad, the best model of humanity . The above verse from Mawlânâ also emphasizes this truth.

The impact of the Prophet Muhammad's (ﷺ) character on people and his being a role model to all humanity has never ceased to embrace all humanity since his blessed mission. Even those who did not believe in him had to admit the high morals and excellence of the Prophet, while those who loved him sang of their fondness and affection for him. The Companions revealed their submission and devotion by such things as, "I willingly sacrifice all my possessions, my life and loved ones for you." The caravans of affection, which will continue until the Day of Judgment, flow with his love. The universe has been enlightened by his radiance, which is brighter than the sun. The graceful joy of belief is only possible through him. Mortals have not been able to describe him adequately because, with his impeccable morality and existence, he is the unique gem of this universe. Poets and

---

19. Ibn 'Abbâs (ﷺ) implies by this that it is impossible to retaliate against his instigator since this would mean harming a fellow brother-in-faith, an act which his heart simply will not permit (translator).

literary figures have not been able to cease praising him. Here are some of those pearls, verses of beautiful poems that have been sung about him.

The following are from Yaman Dede, a poet who lived in recent times; he was a Christian who chose to become a Muslim after discovering the truth brought by Prophet Muhammed (ﷺ).

I would not feel despair if I were without water in the heat of the desert.

I have volcanoes in my heart that oceans cannot quench.

If it were to rain flames and I touched them, I would not feel it.

Give me some solace with your beauty, I am ablaze O, Rasûlallâh!

What prosperity to close my eyes with your love and to die!

Is it not possible to give my last breath in your circle?

As my eyes fade, it would be easy to die with you, alas!

Give me some solace with your beauty, I am ablaze O. Rasûlallâh!

Muhammad Es'ad Erbili, who was one of the important sufis of recent history, states his compassion for the Prophet (ﷺ) in the following beautiful words:

O, the beloved! From the appearance of your beauty through manifestations,

The spring is ablaze, the rose is ablaze, the hyacinth is ablaze, the earth and   the thorn are ablaze.

What sets the blaze is the light (nûr) of your blessed visage.

(This is why) the soul is ablaze, the heart is ablaze and these two eyes, that are weeping with your affection, are ablaze.

Is it possible to cause the martyr of love take ablution with this many flames?

The body is ablaze, the shroud is ablaze, even the sweet water for washing the martyr is ablaze

It is as if every thing of beauty has caught a reflection of the Prophet's own beauty. This garden of creation has never seen a rose like his face. Fuzûlî describes this truth in his famous "Water Eulogy":

O, Eye! Do not spill your tears onto my heart, which is on fire (with the love of the Messenger of Allah)! Because it is no solace to pour water onto fires that burn with the heat of love. (This fire of love cannot be put out. The drop of water that falls into a burning fire will only increase its flames).

The gardener should not trouble himself to water this rose garden.

Indeed, even if he waters a thousand rose gardens, (O, Messenger of Allah) no rose like your visage will ever open there…

Again Fuzûlî restrains this magnificent yearning to a couplet:

I bleed from my eyes against your visage, which is like a rose.

O, Beloved, this is the season of roses, will it not obscure the flowing water?

The Mathnawi: *"If one person had known what the Prophet knew, they would neither find tenacity for supplication and pleading nor any strength for fasting and prayers."* (v. 2: 1913)

There are three categories of reality, or *haqîqa*, which were bestowed upon the Prophet. Those that are in the first category are kept as an *eternal secret* between Allah Almighty and the Prophet. The Noble Messenger did not reveal even the smallest portion of these to anyone. When explaining this he said:

"I swear by Allah that if you knew what I knew you would weep much and laugh little, you would find no comfort in your wives and you would pour forth onto roads and deserts crying (and calling) to Allah (for him to lift the calamities off you)" (Ibn Mâjah, *Zuhd*, 19)

The *haqîqa* in this category can only be comprehended with the light of Prophethood (*nûr al-nubuwwa*). No one but the Messenger himself has this ability, so this knowledge is an eternal mystery. This matter is from among knowledge which has been left undisclosed.

The second category which was made known to the Prophet was transferred only to a limited number of people who had an exceptional understanding and perception. This knowledge was not meant for the general public. We know that the Prophet spoke to Abû Bakr and 'Alî about some of this. We also know that he entrusted some secrets to Abû Hurayra (ﷺ) and Hudhayfa al-Yamân (ﷺ). The secrets disclosed in this category constitute the foundations of tasavvuf, that is God-given knowledge of *spiritual life*. For this reason, Sufi orders ultimately trace themselves back to Abû Bakr or 'Alî. Knowledge in this category is reserved for the spiritual elite (*khawâs*). This knowledge has been passed down from heart to heart and will continue to be until the Day of Judgment. The information from this category which has found itself in some books is merely the outer peel of the fruit. The essence is not, in fact, "uttered" but is only a "state"; it is not words but nature.

The third category of information given to the Prophet by Allah Almighty is for the masses. These are the canonical laws. The addressees of this information are human beings; the Prophet has not been sent to a particular people or period, but rather he has been appointed as the Messenger for all of humanity. For this reason, from the time he was given his mission until the Day of Judgment, all of humanity is known as the "Community (*Ummah*) of Muhammad". This group is divided into two: those who accept the honoured invitation (*da'wa*) are called *Ummat al-ijâba* (those who respond) and those who reject it are called *Ummat al-ghayr al-ijâba* (those who do not respond) or *Ummat al-da'wa* (those who should be invited). The invitation is for all of humanity.

Rûmî explains these facts in the above verses and goes on to elucidate that being aware of the information in the first category is beyond the strength and capability of humanity.

The Mathnawi: *"The Prophet said: O, my companions! O, my Ummah! Upon you, I am more compassionate and merciful than a father."*

The Prophet's love for his *Ummah* is of course much stronger and greater when compared to a father's affection for his children. The biographies (*sîra*) of the Prophet are full of historical manifestations of this. There are thousands of examples that could be mentioned. He did not eat or drink whilst his *Ummah* remained hungry. He even tied a stone to his stomach to suppress his hunger. If he heard a child crying while in congregational prayer, he would cut the prayer short and read from the shorter chapters of the Qur'ân. He led his *Ummah* at the most difficult of times. He defended his position when the army was defeated at 'Uhud and Hunayn left exposed to the enemy lines. During some campaigns he stayed behind and helped the army to gather the troops. His devotion to his *Ummah* is explained as follows in the Qur'ân:

"Indeed, there has come unto you [O mankind] an Apostle from among yourselves: it heavily weighs upon him [the thought] that you might suffer [in the life to come]; full of concern for you [is he, and] full of compassion and mercy towards the believers." (Tawba, 9: 128)

In this verse, Allah Almighty extols the Prophet (ﷺ) with the titles *Ra'ûf* and *Rahîm*, attributes that belong to Allah.

With his actions, words and morality the Prophet (ﷺ) was a guide and a mercy who embraced all of humanity. On the way of guidance, the greatest difficulties and tribulations rested on his shoulders. He accomplished his divine duty flawlessly. He possessed such a state of patience and ardor that sometimes he received Divine instruction not to exhaust himself.

This lofty virtue shown by the Prophet (ﷺ) for the salvation of humanity is stated in the following verse:

"Wouldst thou, perhaps, torment thyself to death [with grief] because they [who live around thee] refuse to believe [in it]?" (Shu'arâ, 26: 3)

The Manners of
the Prophet

THE MANNERS OF THE PROPHET

*T*he attainment of morals and religion are the only preconditions for living in a way that is befitting to humanity. Allah Almighty sent the Prophet Muhammad (ﷺ), an example of morals without equal, to mankind so that they would be able to live a life of faith and adoration on the straight path. The Messenger's main duties, after instructing us in the faith, were to save believers from their egotistical characteristics and to elevate them in praiseworthy characteristics.

The one sent as an example for mankind by Allah as the Messenger of Islam, the perfected religion, was Prophet Muhammad (ﷺ). Allah Almighty revealed the following about him: *"Surely thou hast sublime morals...!"* (Qalam, 68: 4) Thus, the only way to assure prosperity in this world and the next is to benefit from the example given by the character, life and excellent conduct of the Prophet Muhammad (ﷺ). We can only attain this blessing with affection for the Prophet Muhammad (ﷺ) and by enfolding ourselves in his spirituality.

The universe is the manifestation of Divine love. The true essence of this manifestation is the light of Muhammad (ﷺ).

Happiness in this world and the next can be attained only with love that we feel for him. History is a witness that prosperity comes to a nation when it adorns itself with love for the Prophet of Islam. We can only preserve the infinite grace, aesthetic beauty and unseen depths that we humans have been so generously created with by obeying Allah and living according to the Prophet Muhammad's morals and high standards.

Rûmî tells us about a person during the *asr-i saadet*[20] who lost his conscience, whose feelings were stricken with atrophy, and who was impolite and abrupt; he then goes on to tell us how the Prophet Muhammad (ﷺ) gracefully dealt with the situation and how he helped this man to find faith.

One evening a few unbelievers came to the mosque as guests of the Prophet and said: "O blessed one, who spiritually hosts all of mankind! We have come here as your guests. We have nothing to eat or drink; we have come from afar and we know of nobody here. Come and show us your grace and goodness, spread your light, give of your prosperity, your kindness and favour."

The Prophet Muhammad (ﷺ) said to his Companions: "O Friends! Divide these people between you and take them to your homes, give them offerings, because you are like me with generosity and you have my morals." The Companions all took a guest to their home. However, there was one among them who was not like the others; a rude man who was obese. Nobody had the courage to take this man to their home. He was left alone in the mosque so the Prophet Muhammad (ﷺ) took the man to his home.

There were seven goats in the Prophet's herd which provided milk. At dinner time the goats were outside waiting to

---

20. The era of happiness:

be milked. The large guest ate all the bread and food and drank the milk of the seven goats. Some members of the household were very annoyed with this insensitive, rude man because he had eaten all the food in the house. The man's stomach swelled like a drum; he ate the food of seven or eight people on his own. At night time he retired to another room and a servant girl resented the man so much that she secured the door with a chain from the outside.

During the night, however, the guest had a stomach ache and needed to leave the room. He flew out of bed and ran to the door. When he tried to open the door he realized that it had been chained from the outside. This glutton of a man tried to open the door in many ways, and he kept on trying, but all in vain; the door would not open. He was so desperate to relieve himself that the room seemed to start to close in on him, but there was nothing he could do, no remedy or comfort...so he lay down and tried to sleep to forget his discomfort. He fell asleep and in his dream he saw himself in a place of desolation. There was a ruined house which he remembered from long ago. Seeing himself in the secluded house he took this opportunity and relieved himself in the corner of the room. He was so ashamed when he woke up to see that he had soiled the bed that he was sleeping in. He waited, thinking to himself 'I hope the night passes quickly and I hear the door open soon.' He waited so that he could rush out of the door as soon as it opened.

In the morning the Prophet Muhammad (ﷺ) came and opened the door to let the man out, but the man hid with shame. As soon as he found a chance he ran off. A member of the household later brought the bedding and placed it in front of the Prophet Muhammad (ﷺ), as if to say "look at what your guest has done." The merciful one just smiled and said:

"Bring me a bowl of water and I'll wash the bedding with my own hands." All the people in the room jumped up, ashamed and said: "No we'll do it. Leave the filth and we will clean it. This is work for the hand, not the heart. We are here to serve you. If you do our duties, then what are we? What duty do we serve?" Prophet Muhammad (ﷺ) replied: "I know how much you all love me, but there is a wisdom in my washing this." The members of the household then waited for the wisdom to be revealed.

The Prophet (ﷺ) washed the filth because he was in fact complying with an order from Allah; this is what his blessed soul had told him to do. As it turned out, there was a great deal of wisdom in all of this, for the unbelieving man who stayed at the Prophet's home had had an idol around his neck. When he realized that he had lost it, he said to himself: "I must have dropped my valuable idol in the room without realizing it." He was so ashamed of what he had done, but the value of the lost idol allowed him to overcome his shame.

He ran back to look for his idol. He located the idol in the Prophet Muhammad's room, but he also saw the Prophet; the blessed hand of Allah's power, washing the sheets he had dirtied. All the affection he had for the idol vanished from his heart, and realizing what he had done he fell into a state of ecstasy; he tore at his clothes, hit his face and head with his hands and banged his head against the wall and the door, saying: "O, you stupid head!", beating his chest and saying "O you chest of no splendour!", bowing down to the ground and shouting, "You pitiful person of no conscience!"

Then the man said: "O Glory of the Universe, honourable person of divinity! I'm ashamed of the heedlessness I have shown to your kindness." Talking to the earth from a stricken soul he said: "O earth, full of wisdom! You abide by the command of Allah and bow to Him. You live with His love, while I am just a pitiful person who thrives on the blessings you adorn. I have been defeated by my ego and I am out of control. When you face Allah you are humble and powerless, that is why you tremble when you praise him. As for me, I have opposed His orders. Shame on me!"

Looking up to the heavens, the man said to the Prophet Muhammad: "O *qibla* of the universe! I have no right to look you in the face." His state of ecstasy had gone too far, he was trembling and in a fluster. The Prophet Muhammad (ﷺ) took this poor person who was trying to flee from disbelief, and restored him with peace, reviving his heart that was in ruins. He spoke to the man with words of deep mystery. This man who had been captivated by his idol had never seen a heart like the one which was standing in front of him, a heart of kindness and morals; the two men soon became close friends. The Prophet (ﷺ) was surprised that the abrupt, arrogant man had turned into a person of immense humility. The Prophet Muhammad (ﷺ) told the man to come over to him. As if he had just awoken from a deep sleep, the man went over to the Prophet and said: "O witness of the unity of Allah, teach me the testimony of unification: faith to the oneness of Allah and verification of your Prophethood, then I will be able to join the caravan of happiness. I am wearied by my abruptness, of my conscience not having any feeling. I want to reach the eternal desert of faith."

The Prophet Muhammad (ﷺ) instructed the man in faith. He taught to him the holy words of testimony: "*Lâ ilâha illallâh, Muhammad'ur Rasûllallâh.*" Prophet Muhammad (ﷺ) said to the man: "Come to us tonight and be the guest of our home and our hearts." The fortunate man said: "I swear that whatever

I am or wherever I go I will be your guest forever. I was dead but you revived me. I am your free servant from now on, your doorman. Everyone, in this world and in the Hereafter, they are all your guests."

That night, the Bedouin was again a guest of the Prophet Muhammad (ﷺ); he only drank a small amount of the milk from one of the goats and then he thanked Allah for what he had eaten and got up. The Prophet Muhammad (ﷺ) said to him: "Drink some milk and eat." The newcomer to faith replied: "I swear I am truly full; I am not just saying this out of shame or embarrassment, nor am I saying it just for show. One mouthful of your prosperity is worth hundreds of mouthfuls. I am fuller than I was last night after eating all that food."

The members of the household were surprised, and speaking amongst themselves, said: "How can a man of his size be full on a drop of olive oil?" "How can the food fit for a swallow fill an elephant's stomach? How surprising it is that a man with a body like an elephant is eating something the size of a mosquito!" In reality, after being saved from the contempt of disbelief, the stomach of a dragon can be filled by the food for an ant.

This story contains much wisdom; first of all, a guide must teach moral values to the person who is on the path. Implementing and displaying these morals within his own self, the Prophet Muhammad (ﷺ) took the overeating disbeliever that nobody else wanted to his house as a guest, he fed him and showed him overwhelming kindness; he even gave the man his own share of the food. When the man was forced to soil the sheets, Prophet Muhammad (ﷺ) cleaned up after him and this action caused the man to admire the Prophet's morals; he cleaned up what the servants had found hard to clean. The Prophet (ﷺ) never criticized the man. With great maturity the

Prophet Muhammad (ﷺ) displayed a heart of loyalty. As a result of this, the heedless, greedy man, who had a heart of darkness, was filled with the light of faith. It was the conduct of the Prophet Muhammad (ﷺ) that caused this man to see the light and redeem his past mistakes. This is the conduct of a Prophet!

- This conduct can make a disbeliever a believer, and a glutton an ocean of contentment.

- This conduct can make many rampant souls obedient and turn cold-blooded hearts into oceans of compassion.

- This conduct can make a savage society into the most refined community in humanity.

- This conduct can make people hold themselves responsible for all their negative qualities.

- This conduct can instruct in good and beautification with kindness, because it is kindness that overcomes humans. To whatever degree we show kindness that is the degree to which hostility will fade and those left behind will become friends. It is stated in the Qur'ân: *"Repel evil with that which is better…!"* (Muminûn, 23: 96; Fussilat, 41: 34)

- This conduct made the Prophet Muhammad the sultan of two universes.

- This conduct is the highest divine conduct that pleases Allah: *"Surely thou hast sublime morals."* (Qalam, 68: 4)

O Allah! Beautify our manners with the manners of the Prophet Muhammad. His actions are full of eternal beauty; grant all those of faith the ability to live with the same conduct as the Holy Prophet! Âmîn!

Neither offending
Nor being offended I.

NEITHER OFFENDING NOR BEING OFFENDED I.

*T*he **Mathnawi:** *"If you know who is within this heart, what is this rude behavior at the front door of the Owner of the heart?"*

"Ignorant ones show respect to man-made masjids, but through apathy they break the tender hearts." (v.2: 3108-3109)

The heart is under the constant gaze of the Lord Almighty. Wounding a heart is the greatest offence a *nafs* can commit. For this reason in a couplet Mawlânâ says:

*"Kâ'be bünyâd-ı Halîl-i Âzer est
Dil, nazargâh-ı Celîl-i Ekber est"*

The meaning is that the Ka'ba is a structure that was built by Ibrâhîm, the son of Âzar, but the heart is the place where Allah Almighty's gaze falls. Therefore, demolishing a heart, which is a place where the Almighty gazes, is a greater sin than demolishing the Ka'ba.

In addition, Yûnus Emre, the well-known Turkish dervish and poet, points out the same fact:

The old hodja with a white beard
Is not aware of his state (his place in front of Allah).
He should not trouble himself with the Hajj
If he has broken a heart.

The human being is the most honored of creation and has been created as the most perfect of all. A human heart is the site at which Allah Almighty gazes. In a *hadîth qudsî* Allah Almighty says, *"Neither the earth nor the heavens will contain Me; only the heart of the believing servant (contains me)."* (Ajlûnî, *Kashfu l-Khafâ*, II: 195) All this further clarifies the honored state of humans and the gravity of hurting another human or wounding their hearts.

Those with a wounded heart have a highly esteemed place with Allah Almighty. Those who wish to please Allah should gratify these sad souls. Indeed, one day the Prophet Mûsâ (علیه السلام) made a supplication to Allah Almighty and said:

"O Lord! Where shall I seek for you?" Allah Almighty replied, *"Seek me with those whose hearts have been broken!"* (Abû Nu'aym, Hilya, II; 364)

In a *hadîth qudsî* narrated from Abû Hurayra (رضي الله عنه), the beloved Prophet (ﷺ) said, *"On the day of resurrection Allah, the Azîz and the Jalîl, will say, 'O Mankind! I was unwell, did you visit me?' The servant will answer, 'O Lord! When You are the Lord of the heavens and earth how can I visit You?' Allah Almighty will reply, 'You knew that such and such a servant of mine was ill, yet you did not visit him. Do you not know that if you had visited him you would have found Me with him?'*

Allah Almighty will say, 'O Mankind! I wanted food from you but you did not feed me!' The servant will reply, 'O Lord, how can I feed You? You are the Lord of the Universe!' Allah

Almighty will say, 'Such and such a servant of mine wanted food from you. You did not feed him. Do you not know that if you had given him food you would have found Me with him!' Allah Almighty will say, 'O Mankind! I wanted water from you but you did not give me water!' The servant will answer, 'O Lord! How can I give water to you? You are the Lord of the Worlds!' Allah Almighty will reply, 'Such and such a servant of mine wanted water from you. You did not give him water. Do you not know that if you had given him water you would have found Me with him!'" (Muslim, *Birr*, 43)

Regardless of being a Muslim or a heathen, the prayer of every person who has been hurt or who is under oppression is presented to Allah Almighty and accepted in the shortest time. Indeed, there are no barriers between the prayers of a wronged person and Allah Almighty. The Messenger of Allah advised the Companions to avoid the curses of these wronged people whose prayers are guaranteed saying:

"Beware of the curse of the wronged person because there are no barriers between him and the Lord Almighty." (Muslim, *Imân*, 29)

"There are three people whose prayers will not be rejected by Allah: 1. The prayer of the fasting person until they break their fast; 2. The prayer of the wronged person; 3. The prayer of a just ruler." (Tirmidhî, *Da'awât*, 48; Ibn Mâjah, *Du'â*, 2)

The following *hadîth* beautifully expresses that Allah Almighty will not permit His servants to be despised: The Messenger of Allah (ﷺ) told us: "[Once] a man abruptly said, *'I swear by Allah that He will not forgive such and such a person.'* The Lord Almighty replied, *'Who is the one swearing that I will not forgive such and such a person? I*

have forgiven him and cancelled all of your (good) deeds!'"
(Muslim, *Birr*, 137)

The Mathnawi: *"Allah will not wreak ruin upon a people unless they hurt a Prophet, a saint or a godly person"* (v.2: 3112)

The couplet states that one of the main reasons for the destruction of a people is that they have hurt a Prophet or a person close to Allah. This also means that individuals or groups that respect, value and esteem those who are close to Allah will be rewarded with an increase in their honor and dignity.

In a *hadîth al-qudsî* it is said, *"Whosoever shows enmity to someone devoted to Me, I shall be at war with him. My servant draws not near to Me with anything more loved by Me than the religious duties I have enjoined upon him, and My servant continues to draw near to Me with supererogatory works so that I shall love him. When I love him, I am his hearing with which he hears, his seeing with which he sees, his hand with which he strikes, and his foot with which he walks. Were he to ask (something) of Me, I would surely give it to him, and were he to ask Me for refuge, I would surely grant him it.."* (Bukhârî, *Riqâq*, 38)

Few better examples than Mûsâ (﷽) exist in this regard.. Recognizing his sublime and spiritual power, the magicians of the Pharaoh asked him if he would like to be the first to throw his staff. Thus, with the *barakah* (blessing) of this kindness, as they had accepted the supremacy of a person who was close to Allah, they were blessed with guidance. On the other hand, they were requited with a punishment for their audacity in competing with a Prophet. As we know, they were first tortured and then martyred, their hands and feet cut off on the order of the Pharaoh.

Whilst in competition with Mûsâ the magicians had reached the lowest point of *kufr* (disbelief) yet on the very same day they managed to reach the highest spiritual heights from where they defied the Pharaoh; when faced by his oppression and menace they were able draw from the level of their *îmân* such that they preferred the eternal to the transient.

"They (magicians) answered, "Never shall we prefer thee to all the evidence of the truth that has come unto us, nor to Him who has brought us into being! Decree, then, whatever thou art going to decree: thou canst decree only [something that pertains to] this worldly life!" (Tâhâ, 20: 72)

In another verse of the Qur'ân we are told,

"They answered, "No harm [canst thou do to us]: verily, unto our Sustainer do we turn!" (Shu'arâ, 26: 50)

Worried about the weakening of their *îmân* as the Pharaoh severely tortured them, they pleaded with Allah for steadfastness in patience and *îmân*.

"O our Sustainer! Shower us with patience in adversity, and make us die as men who have surrendered themselves unto Thee!" (A'râf, 7: 126)

Rûmî analyses the spiritual dimension of this event as follows: *"The cursed and tyrannical Pharaoh, threatening the magicians because of their îmân, said, 'I will have your hands and feet cut off (alternately) and then I will not forgive you, but have you hanged.' The Pharaoh thought that the magicians would be frightened and startled, bowing down before him trembling. But the Pharaoh did not know that the magicians were free of fear and worry, and were aware of Divine secrets and truth. Even if they were beaten a hundred times and became powder in the mortars of fate, they now had the wisdom and foresight to differentiate their shadows from themselves."*

This means that the magicians understood that the soul is the reality and the body is but a shadow. They sacrificed this shadow immediately and reached the state of *fanâfillah*.

"O mankind! This world is but a resting place and a dream. Do not be taken in by the merriment and splendor of it. Even if your hand is cut off or if you are sliced into pieces in a dream, do not be frightened! The Prophet Muhammad (May God bless him and grant him peace) said, 'This world is naught but a dream.'"

The Mathnawi: *"Some people attempted to struggle against the Prophets. They saw their bodies (the Prophets' bodies) and thought them to be ordinary people."* (v.2: 3113)

Those who regard Prophets to be like their fellow beings and do not see the Divine manifestations, the wisdom and the privileges that have been bestowed upon them cannot save their *nafs* from being dragged into erroneous actions or impiety. This is a state that has existed throughout history. People who could not perceive the Prophets, their divine duties or their complete spiritual worlds have been ruined because of their audacity and because they are unable to attain submission or obedience. The likes of Abû Jahl and Abû Lahab thought of the Prophet Muhammad as mere flesh and blood, no different to themselves; as a result they were destroyed for their inability to comprehend.

The Companions who knew the Prophet well observed him in awe. Abû Bakr (ﷺ) who was one of the most prominent of the Companions, felt a yearning for the Prophet even when they were together; he closely observed the Messenger, the sun to both worlds, with admiration.

119

The state of the Prophet's muezzin, Bilâl (ﷺ), was a different story. When the Messenger of Allah passed away, it was as if Bilâl had lost his voice unable to speak. He could not stay in Medina any longer.

Abû Bakr the Caliph pleaded with him to call the prayer once more, but Bilâl's answer was: "O Abû Bakr! Ask me what I wish for I do not have the strength to call the prayer after the death of the Messenger of Allah. Do not force me. Please let me be..." But Abû Bakr wanted to hear once more the beautiful call to prayer of which rung out in the days of old; he continued pleading with Bilâl finally saying, "After being deprived of their Messenger, should the nation be deprived of the Messenger's muezzin too?" Bilâl (ﷺ) finally gave in and went up the minaret, trying his utmost to hold back his tears, in order to make the call for the morning prayer. He could not contain himself, however, and began to weep. Bilâl, unable to bring himself to make the call, in spite of all efforts, was pressed no further by Abû Bakr in this regard.

Bilâl could not stay in Medina any longer and the same morning he immediately left for the city of Damascus. He participated in battles on the frontiers so that he would become a martyr and be with the Messenger of Allah; but as a matter of Divine predestination, he returned alive after each battle. Years passed in such a state.

One night, he saw the Messenger in his dream. The Messenger said to him, "O Bilâl! What is this pain? Is it not time for you to visit me?"

Bilâl woke up in haste and immediately set off into the desert on his camel. After traveling on his own for many days, he at last reached the radiant city of Medina. He ran straight to the grave of the Prophet before anyone could catch sight of him, and collapsed on the grave upon reaching it. As he put his head on the grave he started to cry and said, "I have come, O Messenger, I have come!" Just at that moment the Prophet's grandsons Hasan and Hussayn (صلى الله عليه وسلم) came. Seeing them, Bilâl rose and embraced them tightly, saying, "O the lights of the Prophet's eyes!" Hasan said, "Bilâl, I would like to ask you something, but will you do it for me?" Bilâl responded, "Tell me, my dear child, tell me!" Hasan said, "We long to hear you make the call to prayer as you once did for the Prophet at his masjid. We would like to hear it, will you make it?" "I will make it for you," replied Bilâl. At noon, Bilâl went up to the place where he used to make the call to prayer in the masjid of the Prophet. He began to shout *"Allâhu Akbar, Allâhu Akbar!"* in such a way that all of Medina shook associating this sound with the Messenger of Allah. The mountains and rocks wailed with this deep cry. When Bilâl reached *"Ash hadu an lâ ilâha ilallâh"* the whole city trembled and with *"Ashhadu anna Muhammadan Rasâlallâh!"* everyone poured onto the streets. People were asking each other if the Messenger had returned to the world; people were crying, wailing…

Bilâl (صلى الله عليه وسلم) was trying to not choke on his tears in order to complete the call. But it was not possible… He could not contain himself; he was exhausted and fainted on the spot.

Sayyidina Fâtimah (عليها السلام), the most esteemed of the women of Heaven, was another soul who was deeply grieved by the passing away of her father, the Messenger of Mercy. "The passing of the Messenger to the afterlife was such a calamity for me that if it had come at the time of darkness, the color of darkness would have changed."

121

May Allah enlighten our hearts with the love of the beloved Prophet, the Companions and the people of God who follow in their footsteps. May He enable us to know the Prophet well and benefit from his character and personality. May He make the Prophet's sublime love a sustenance for our hearts, one which never is exhausted, but increases continuously! Âmîn!

The Mathnawi: "*When in anger, if you have wounded hearts and caused them to burn, that fire will feed the hellfire for you*"

"*The fire of your anger will burn you even in this world; it will cause you destruction. The hellfire born from this destruction will burn you eternally in the Hereafter.*"

"*Here, the fire of your rage is aimed at people. The fire of Hell, which is the end product of this aim, will attack you eternally in the Hereafter.*" (v.3: 3472-3474)

The perfect man has such an impeccable morality and nature that he is not angry with anyone or hurt by anyone. He has reached the secret of the following verse:

"*The God conscientious- who spend [in His way] in time of plenty and in time of hardship, and hold in check their anger, and pardon their fellow-men because God loves the doers of good;*" (Âl 'Imrân, 3: 134)

It is narrated that Ja'far al-Sâdiq (﷽) had a slave who took care of the domestic chores. One day, the slave accidentally poured a bowl of soup over Ja'far. Ja'far, covered in soup, looked angrily at the slave's face. The slave said, "Sir! In the Qur'ân it says, '…those who defeat their anger," to which Ja'far replied, "I have defeated my anger!" This time the slave said, "In the same place of the Qur'ân it says, "…those who pardon their fellow men." Ja'far said, "Alright! I forgive you!" But the slave continued, "At the end of the ayah it says, "Allah loves the doers of good." After this Ja'far said, "All right, you are now free; I have freed you for the sake of Allah!"

The chapter of anger from the book of life is in fact a history of disaster. The remedy against these despised outbursts of rage, the way to deliverance from this grave danger, is to use the strength of brotherhood and patience, and, without disturbing the balance, to enwrap oneself in silence.

When Abû Dardâ (﷦) asked the Prophet (ﷺ) to teach him something that would take him to Heaven, the Prophet replied, "Do not get angry!" (Bukhârî, *Adab*, 76; Tirmidhî, *Birr*, 73)

On another occasion a person came to the Prophet (ﷺ) and said, "O, Messenger of Allah, I do not have the strength to memorize a great deal. Tell me something concise which will bring true happiness." The Prophet (ﷺ) also told him, "Do not get angry." In other *hadîths* it is said, "Allah Almighty will cover the shameful acts of those who hold their anger" (*Ihyâ*, III, 372) "There is no deed better for a servant than containing his anger in order to attain the blessings of Allah." (*Ihyâ*, III, 392) "The strong and powerful wrestler is not the one who throws everyone, pinning them to the floor. The real hero is the one who holds his anger in at the appropriate time." (Bukhârî, *Adab*, 102; Muslim, *Birr*, 106-108)

The Mathnawi: *"If a weak and miserable person asks for the mercy and help of Allah Almighty, a great clamor will fall onto the armies of the Heavens (i.e. the angels)."* (vol. 1: 1315)

"O man! The oppression and wickedness you see from others are the reflection and the manifestation of your own bad behavior which is only emanating from them." (vol. 1: 1318)

In one *hadîth* we are warned against the complaints of the oppressed and it is said that nothing can stand in the way of their prayers reaching the Divine Presence. Therefore, one should refrain from oppressing others. However, the oppressed should also think that the oppression and wickedness they face are a reflection and manifestation of their own bad character in another person. Thus, Mawlâna describes the peace and restlessness in a person's inner and outer worlds as follows:

"If a thorn has pricked you, know that you planted that thorn! If you rest within soft and beautiful materials, know that you have woven them!"

"If you were to delve into the depths of your character and nature you would know that wickedness and immorality comes from yourself."

However, all the misfortune and bad treatment one faces are not always a result of one's own faults. If this were so, the Prophets, who are without sin, would never have encountered ill-treatment. These misfortunes are sometimes an integral part of this world, which is a place of trial, and sometimes are aimed at helping a person mature spiritually.

Nevertheless, some misfortunes come because of the actions of people themselves, as mentioned above; in such cases, one should check and account for one's actions. For this reason, before talking, we should be careful about what comes out of our mouths. The intention should not be to hurt with the thorns that fall from our dagger, but to shield hearts within our own heart. Our behavior should reflect what we say and we should reflect this beauty all around us.

The Mathnawi: *"One who hurts a human does not know that he has hurt Allah. Does he not know that the water in*

this pitcher is mingled with the water of the river of Haqq?"
(vol. 1: 2520)

Offending a believer will bring Allah's anger even before such a behavior causes that person's anger. This is because Allah loves His creation very much. Hence He even forbids backbiting His sinner slave in order to protect that person's honor.

The Lord Almighty has given mankind an aptitude for drawing close to Him, as He has stated in the following verse: *"... I breathed into him of My spirit (i.e. of my qudra)..."* (Hijr, 15: 29, Sâd, 38: 72) and He created the human with the secret of *ahsan al-taqwîm* in the finest form. For this reason, Allah Almighty does not approve of any of His servants being hurt through disparagement or belittling. It is said that as he was crossing a beach, Muhyiddîn Ibn 'Arabî saw a young man drinking wine from a jug. The same man was also laughing loudly with a woman next to him. Muhyiddîn Ibn 'Arabî thought to himself, "A human must think himself the lowest of creation and be very humble, but I think I am superior to this young sinner. I do not drink wine and I do not act in a way that is reckless or immoral." Just then, a cry was heard from the sea," We are sinking, help!" Hearing this cry, the young man threw the jug and ran into the sea in an instant; in a couple of minutes he was carrying four people who had nearly drowned onto the beach. Ibn 'Arabî, who was watching everything that took place in astonishment, had found the answer to his doubts which had earlier arisen in his mind. He thought, "Look, that young man who you so belittled and despised, thinking him a sinner, has saved four people in an instant. What did you do? You were not even able to save one!"

As in this anecdote, there will exist people who we can only see outwardly, yet who conceal within talents and treasures. There is no guarantee for anyone concerning their last breath except for the Prophets. For this reason, the people of *tasawwuf* have acknowledged that belittling the servants of Allah is like murdering the heart.

The Mathnawi: "*You become angry with every difficulty, you spite every rude person. Well then, how will you become a mirror without being polished?*" (vol. 1: 2980)

A human being matures through difficulties and deprivation. Avoiding every difficulty is a means of indolence, selfishness and a weakness of the mind. The correct thing to do is to look and see if there is a balance between the difficulty one is enduring and the result one will achieve.

According to this measure, a person who faces treatment that they have not deserved should question themselves to see if they have in some way called for this, rather than getting angry and retaliating. When treated badly, even when one does not deserve it, showing patience is the first level of maturity, and being thankful and feeling sorry for the perpetrator is the highest level. Such strength is rare and is by no means easy. Such strong wrestlers are really few in number.

Having compassion and being close to the weak, the poor, the wretched and the lonely is a requisite of mercy. But one should feel pity also towards

– **"The conscience of the oppressors"** that persecute the helpless and weak people.

– **"Wretched souls who enslave"** their vast opportunities for the **"splendor of mortal and excessive pleasure"**,

– **"Vile souls who are destitute of mercy"** in an environment where rights and justice are absent. Because, these people will be the greatest losers in the Hereafter.

The story of Habîb al-Najjâr, which we read in verses thirteen to twenty-seven of Yâsîn is a beautiful example that demonstrates the heroic dimension of this attitude. Habîb al-Najjâr was martyred because he informed people about the truth. According to the Qur'ânic declaration, as he was saying farewell to life, the divine curtains were parted before his eyes and he said, *"Would that my people knew how my Sustainer has forgiven me [the sins of my past], and has placed me among the honored ones!"* (Yâsîn, 36: 26-27)

The one who martyred himself as a sign of his closeness to Allah felt pity for the heedlessness and misery of his people.

Al Mathnawi: *"The important thing is to have the temperament of a rose. Which in this garden of the world means rather than seeing the thorns and being hurt by them, thus becoming like a thorn, one should be like a rose for the entire world, embracing them with the mood of spring, even though trials such as winter come in between."* (v.3: 3259)

For a human being, becoming a rose means becoming *"good (khayr) itself"*. People who can achieve this are even able to make snakes submissive. This is because those who are close to Allah never look at any of Allah's creation with enmity (*bughd*) or hatred. The natural animosity they feel against evil is the object of a secrecy that goes beyond the evil-doer. This is called *bughd fillâh*, that is "being angry for the sake of Allah".

It is not easy to have such kind regard and sentiments with the incidents that take place in this world. In order to achieve this, one needs to travel a great distance on the journey, which starts at the *nafs al-ammâra* and ends at the *nafs al-kâmila*.

Mawlânâ converses with the rose in the following fashion:

127

"The rose gained its beautiful smell because it got along well with the thorn. Listen to this truth also from the rose. See what it says: 'Why should I fall into despair because I am with the thorn, why should I let myself grieve? I have gained laughter for bearing togetherness with that ill-natured thorn. Through it I was able to put forth beauties and pleasant scents to the world...'"

In order to have an affect on those one comes across, a believer should reach a maturity in their behavior and language where they will feel responsible for the mistakes of such people. Just like a doctor whose responsibility is to look for a cure for illnesses rather than getting angry with the patient, the people of *tasawwuf* see the sinners as birds with broken wings and instead of getting angry they take them into the courts of their hearts, hating the sin, not the sinner.

Neither offending Nor being offended II.

NEITHER OFFENDING NOR BEING OFFENDED II.

'Abdullah Ibn Umm-i Maktûm (☙), a man blind from birth, was one of the first muezzins of the Prophet Muhammad (☙). He would often visit the Prophet and plead: "O messenger of Allah! Teach me what Allah has taught you!" The Prophet Muhammad would never offend this pure hearted man; rather, he answered all his questions.

One day a few men from the tribe of Quraysh were with the Prophet Muhammad (☙). The Prophet was hopeful that these members of Quraysh would accept the faith and so make it possible for those around them to learn and accept Islam as well. During the course of the meeting, 'Abdullah Ibn Umm-i Maktûm came in. Due to his disability, he did not realize who the Prophet Muhammad (☙) was with; he thus began insisting to be taught. The Prophet was somewhat frustrated at being interrupted by questions whilst he in the process of explaining the religion to his guests. He thus turned his head and ignored 'Abdullah. The blind man became upset at being ignored; this incident became the occasion of revelation for the following two verses:

"(The Prophet) frowned and turned away, because there came to him the blind man (interrupting)." ('Abasa, 80: 1-2)

131

After this incident, whenever the Prophet Muhammad (ﷺ) saw 'Abdullah Ibn-i Maktûm he would say jokingly: "Welcome to the one on whose behalf my Lord rebuked me!" This incident, without doubt, is a divine example of how Allah refined the divine character of the Prophet Muhammad (ﷺ). Not even the slightest harshness was left in the Prophet because he was continually reminded by Allah of his position, and his effect on those soft hearted ones around him. It also stands as an eternal example of how all believers should act in similar circumstances; that of protecting the feelings of everyone, even to the point of not frowning in front of one who cannot see,

The friends of Allah thus became very careful not to offend the feelings of others, not to brake hearts which were considered like a spiritual Ka'ba of Allah; they knew that whoever harms the heart harms the owner of that heart. This is why they say: "Allah is with the broken hearted." Indeed, Moses sought refuge in Allah and asked: "O Allah! Where should I search for you?" Allah Almighty said: "Look for me near the broken hearted ones."

In the following story, related by Mawlânâ, this reality is explained most beautifully:

There was a dervish on a boat; he had no baggage or goods. With good manners, courage and humility he placed his head on a pillow to sleep. While the boat was sailing across the water a pouch of gold went missing. The men on the boat looked everywhere for the gold, but in vain. Then one of the men pointed at the dervish and said: "Search that sleeping crook."

Due to his distress, the owner of the lost money awoke the dervish. He looked at the innocent dervish with accusing eyes and said: "A pouch of gold has gone missing; we've searched everyone but can't find it. Now it's your turn! Take off your cloak and get undressed; prove our doubts to be unfounded." The dervish sought refuge in Allah and said: "O Allah! They accuse your innocent servant. I submit myself to you!"

Those on the boat had acted in a way that hurt the dervish's feelings. Allah Almighty was not pleased that the pure heart of the dervish had been offended. Allah the Merciful at that moment commanded the fish in the sea to emerge from the water; in the mouth of each fish was a valuable pearl. Each pearl was the equivalent to the wealth of an entire nation. Each was a blessing from Allah and belonged to no one.

The dervish took a few of the pearls and threw them into the centre of the boat; he then jumped into the air and crossed his legs like a king. He sat floating in mid air. The boat continued sailing over the sea and the dervish said to those on the boat: "Continue sailing on your boat, let Allah be mine! He neither accuses me of stealing nor abandons me to those who falsely accuse me."

The people on the boat asked: "O noble servant! Why have you been given this exraordinary power?" The dervish answered: "It has been given to me because I respect the friends of Allah and I never think ill about poor people. Ah, these respected poor ones. Surah 'Abasa was sent to glorify them for their poverty. In their world they have nothing but Allah; this is why they embrace poverty."

This has been elegantly expressed by a poet: "*Whoever hurts the heart of the poor, the arrow of Allah will hurt him.*"

Based on this story, Mawlânâ Rûmî wrote these lines:

"*He who offends a person does not realize that he has offended Allah. Such a person does not realize that the*

133

water in this jug (heart) has been mixed with the water of Allah";

"Due to our ignorance and blindness we despise and want to harm the saints of Allah. This is an illness; a call on misfortune. The friends of Allah show sympathy for those who call on this misfortune, but our foolishness is such an illness that it hurts and harms others";

"Foolish people show respect for those who are in the man-made masjid yet offend those who possess hearts."

"If you know who dwells in the home of the heart, then why are you so ill-mannered when at the door of the owner of the heart?"

"But if a man of Allah, a messenger, or a pious one's heart is not offended, then Allah would never disgrace or dishonour a nation."

Tasawwuf places great emphasis on avoiding offending people. An example of one who understood this is Sâmi Efendi. He had just finished the Dâr al-Funûn, Faculty of Law. A saintly companion of Allah who liked Sâmi Efendi's lovely ways and his gleaming soul said to him: "My son, this education is good, but try to complete the real training. Register with the school of wisdom; go and learn the knowledge of the heart and the mysteries of the Hereafter!" The wise man then said: "My son, I do not know how they educate or how they teach; the only thing I know is that the first lesson is not to offend, and the last lesson is not to be offended."

To avoid offending others is relatively easy; as for not being offended, this is not so easy since it is the job of the heart. Not being offended is only possible if the poisonous arrows are blocked before reaching the heart. And this in turn is dependent on the level of purification and perfection of the soul. When the angels saw the Prophet Muhammad being stoned in Ta'if they said:

"O Messenger of Allah! If you like, we will strike these two mountains together and destroy the cruel people who live here."

But the one who was sent as a mercy to mankind, the Prophet Muhammad (ﷺ), did not accept the offer of the angels. In a state of compassion and mercy, he turned his face towards Ta'if and prayed that the community would find the straight path of Islam. It was for this reason that when a lover of the Prophet Muhammad (ﷺ), Hallâj Ibn Mansûr was being stoned, he prayed: "O Allah! They do not know; forgive them before you forgive me!"

Such a heart of perfection can only be achieved with true education and with spiritual discipline. When Abû l-Qâsim al-Hakîm was asked about the attribute of perfection, he said: "The perfection of the heart has three qualities: The first is a heart that offends no one; the second is a heart that is not offended, while the third is kindness, a heart that does everything for the sake of Allah and expects nothing in return. Such a believer will never harm anyone in the presence of Allah because they have true faith. When such a person turns to the Creator without having been offended by anyone they are loyal and when they refrain from telling people of their good deeds then they have a purified soul."

A poet has explained this in the following beautiful way: *"O wise man! If you want to be the favourite of human beings as well as the Jinns; do not allow yourself to be offended and do not let others offend from you."*

One of the most important aspects of not offending or being offended is the covering up of the faults and misconduct of others. Hadrat Hâtem, from the elders of Balkh, achieved this level of understanding to such a degree that, even though he could hear perfectly, he was nicknamed *esamm* or 'the deaf one'. The reason for this nickname is contained in the following story:

One day a woman greatly distressed came with a problem. She had just begun to explain why she had come when then she had a sudden cramp and accidentally passed wind. The woman was so embarrassed that she did not know what to do. So as not to embarrass the woman, Hâtem acted as if he had not heard anything, and, putting his hand to his ear, he said: "Sister, I can't hear you properly. Can you speak bit louder?" Thus the woman thought that her breaking wind had gone unnoticed and relaxed; she was able to explain her problem from the beginning. It was after this incident that Hâtem became known as *Hâtem-i Esamm* (Hâtem the deaf).

It is not possible to apply with ease the covering of faults and similar such manners that are displayed in this story merely from reading them. The show of kindness and consciousness not to offend on Hâtem's part was a feeling received from the compassion and mercy of Allah. Such acts of kindness, particularly in *tasawwuf,* are known as "imbibing the manners of Allah".

The following *hadîth*s are of relevance here: Abû Hurayrah reports that the Prophet said: *"It is a serious evil for a Muslim that he should look down upon his brother Muslim."* (Muslim, 1167); in regards to not taking offence, the Messenger said: *"It is not a virtue to do good to those who have done good or to do bad to those who have done bad; doing good to those who have done bad to you is true virtue."* (Tirmidhî, *Birr*, 63).

Indeed Allah Almighty says: *"The servants of (Allah) most Gracious are those who walk on the earth in humility, and when the ignorant address them, they say, 'Peace!'"* (Furqân, 25: 63)

Achieving these states requires awareness (firasah); people often hurt others without being aware. What is awareness? Awareness is one of the attributes of the Prophets; it means possessing sensitivity and acting, according to the intellectual and psychological level of the person we are talking to. An action that pleases one person could upset another. Therefore, a person achieves politeness by taking another person's state of mind into consideration and by calculating events two or three steps ahead.

Mastering awareness starts when every effort to truly understand death has been made. Being truly aware of the mysteries and the truths of the world is only possible when we understand the meaning of 'death before dying'. It is essential that we abandon the desires of the ego and of this world. The friends of Allah report this in the following code of rules:

Do not forget two things:

1- Allah

2- Death.

Forget two things:

1- Evil that you have encountered

2- Charity and good that you have done.

Forgetting the evil or bad things that have been done to us can be achieved with forgiveness; this is a greater virtue, because a human by forgiving others continuously will deserve the forgiveness of Allah. About such forgiveness, the Qur'ân states:

"Hold to forgiveness; command what is right; but turn away from the ignorant." (A'râf, 7: 199)

"Whether you do openly a good deed or conceal it or cover evil with pardon, surely Allah is ever pardoning Powerful." (Nisâ', 4: 149)

"...let them forgive and overlook: do you not wish that Allah should forgive you?" (Nûr, 24: 22)

Ibn 'Umar related the following to us: "A man came to Prophet Muhammad and asked: 'How many times should I forgive my servant?' The Prophet did not answer him. The man asked again: 'O Messenger of Allah! I asked, how many times should I forgive my servant?' This time the Messenger replied: 'Forgive him seventy times every day!'" (Abu Dawud, 2451). When it was time for the Prophet to depart from this world, he said the following meaningful words: *"The prayer! The prayer! And fear Allah concerning your slaves!"* (Abu Dâwud)

In another *hadîth*, the Messenger (ﷺ) said: *"There was a man of generosity who lent money to the community; he told his servant, 'If you go to collect money that is owed to me from a poor person, but he has no means of paying back the loan, then forgive him (and donate what I gave). May Allah forgive us.' This man was united with Allah and forgiven."* (Bukhârî, *Anbiyâ*, 54; Muslim, *Musâqât*, 31).

These are all explanations of awareness, and for us to act like this is a divine quality that has been placed in our hearts by Allah Almighty. Those who attain this quality become Friends of Allah (Awliyâ); this is why none of the Friends of Allah are foolish. No one who is foolish can rise to the level of being a Companion of Allah.

Whenever the Messenger of Allah praised anyone he would say: "how is his/her understanding/intelligence!" In many different verses Allah Almighty said: *"Have they no intelligence? Will they consider not?"* Allah the Merciful insists that humans use their minds and hearts together. Having the greatest awareness is the key to solving the puzzle of the future. Anyone who solves this puzzle can neither be offended by any mortal person, nor are they able to offend anybody; for in every incident they will be aware of the mystery, the Divine purpose of pre-eternity and post-eternity, and thus will act according to the approval of Allah.

Khâlid of Baghdad relates: "Always be polite to Allah! Never forget that all incidents occur with the permission and planning of Allah. The causes are only temporary vehicles of Divine Will. Sufis say: "Those who know themselves are those who have the following three qualities: 1) They would not even harm the wind; 2) They refrain from speaking of their own qualities; and 3) They approach all that are created by Allah with love and compassion."

In short our level in not offending and not being offended should be;

"The one who comes to kill you should be revived by you." However, the soul must be at a certain stage to be able to achieve this. May Allah Almighty grant everyone a refined and gracious heart of lofty characteristics!

Âmîn!

The Evilness Arrogance (Kibr) in the Mathnawi

THE EVILNESS ARROGANCE (KIBR) IN THE MATHNAWI

*T*he Mathnawi: *"The earth has surrendered to the skies and it says: I am your slave, bring down what you will!"* (vol.3: 452)

"If fire pours onto it from the sun, it turns its face to the fire. Rather than running away from it, it surrenders quietly, spreading its face on the ground against it." (vol. 3: 450)

"O mankind, you are from this earth. You live on it; you should not go against His command, His will or His destiny!"

"You have heard and listened to the verse, "We created you from earth". This means Allah wants you to be like the earth; do not defy the Divine order!"

"Allah says, 'O man! Look carefully and see that I have sown a seed from My soul into your body, which is created from earth. I have exalted you. When you were but dust on this earth I made you a distinguished creature. I gave you intelligence I gave you desire"

142

"Take another step and make the qualities of earth and humbleness an attribute of yourself so that I will render you commander over all My creation." (vol. 3, 453-456)

In the above couplets, Mawlânâ states that humility is an intrinsic trait for a human being and that it is our natural disposition. Since the human body is formed through nourishment that comes from the earth, the origin of the human body is the earth. The soul (*rûh*) stems from the Divine work of Allah Almighty; Mankind is superior to all of creation since it has been elevated to the position of caliph of Allah Almighty by virtue of the *rûh* which enters by Divine breath. Mankind is tasked with becoming as humble as the earth, the source and essence of our bodies. Because of our innate nature, it is natural that we are endowed with the attributes of the earth. When the two abilities of intelligence and volition are used incorrectly, these innate dispositions weaken and become ruined, and as a consequence the human being strays from humility and takes on arrogance, the attribute of the devil. As a result, human beings deviate from their original nature and act against the Divine honour which they carry.

Whatever falls from the heavens, the earth accepts without any objection. Indeed, there is no volition for the earth. In order to reach the zenith of Allah's plan to create this world, mankind should live in submission that is similar to that of the earth before Divine judgement; we should submit to destiny (*qadar*) just as the earth submits without question to the heavens and consents to all that comes from Allah. In this way, man can reach perfection (*kâmâl*) and be considered worthy of the title *Khalifat Allâh,* or caliph of Allah , a position which has been ordained for us on this earth.

The Mathnawi: *"At first the seeds of every fruit lay on the earth. They enter it and then reappear, bursting forth."*

"The origins of all blessings are showered on the earth from the heavens and enter beneath the soil. Then they became life for the pure soul" (vol. 3, 459-460)

The essence or origin of all forms of creation, both the living and the inanimate, is the earth. The transformation of the earth bring about the many varieties in life's forms. The Lord Almighty has covered two-thirds of the earth with water and left only one-third as land. Perhaps only one-third of this land has a surface that is suitable for plant growth. This means, considering the surface area of the world, that only one- sixteenth of the earth is an inexhaustible treasure for the birth of plants, animals and humans, those that have come and those that will come in the future. Allah Almighty has made the earth subject to laws of endless metamorphosis and turned it into the sole provision for these countless bodies. If only one kind of plant or one genus of animal had come to earth since the beginning of time, there would not have been enough space and food for life to continue. As an example, you can think of a pine tree or an elephant. Humans are the same. If all the people were to come into this world at once, they would not be able to find food or a place to step. For this reason, Allah Almighty sends all of His creation to this world in a divine order, through a system of "rotation", using the earth as the essence of His provisions. In that way there is enough space and food for every living being, in its appointed time and place. After living their lifespan they go back to the earth, from where they had come. Life starts from the earth and ends in it.

Since human beings are created from the earth, they carry the earth's characteristics. From time to time the earth dries up, parched from the heat, longing for water. It bears the tribulation of winter for a whole season. Then the time comes for its revival by abundant rainfalls in the spring. The flow of Divine might is displayed with a myriad of beauty, colour, fragrance and harmony. The human is the same. He wavers like desert storms among the passions of life. He destroys himself under the rule of his *nafs*. A human can only reach perfection by overcoming the obstacle of the *nafs*. Just as the earth finds life through the rainfall in the spring, man can reach the point of preferring others over himself through manifestations of *fayz* (knowledge, wisdom, abundance) and *rahmah*. Thus, for the sake of Allah, the human being distributes the blessings that come to him in a state that resembles the beauty and abundance of spring, just like the exuberant earth.

As with the illustration given by Mawlânâ Rûmî of the seed, the plant which grows from it returns to the earth either directly or eventually after passes through several stages. No creation is exempt from this rule. This state is one of the numerous manifestations of Divine magnificence. It is such a great fortune for those who engage in deep meditation. In a verse of the Qur'ân we read:

"Let man consider his food: How We pour water in showers. Then split the earth in clefts. And cause the grain to grow therein and grapes and green fodder and olive-trees and palm-trees and garden-closes of thick foliage and fruits and grasses: Provision for you and your cattle." ('Abasa, 80: 24-32)

The Mathnawi: *"Those with good fortune and who are human know that being clever and trying to be wise are the way of Satan, while 'ashq and servanthood are from the ways of Adam."*

"Those who claim to be clever are like the Satan, they try to survive in the ocean by swimming. It is rare for a person swimming in a vast ocean to survive. In the end, he will sink

and drown. In the end, those who trust their intellect and do board the vessel of Sharî'ah will perish."

"Stop swimming and forgo being conceited, let go of hatred! This water you swim in is not a stream or a river, it is the ocean! This ocean is, in fact, the ocean of qaza and qadar." (v.4: 1402-1404)

Even though Mawlânâ describes the intellect as an attribute that belongs to Shaytân, this is before it receives *tarbiya* (discipline, nurturing and education) through Revelation. Otherwise, the intellect is the principal asset for reaching Allah and good. But this asset alone will not be enough to carry its owner to Allah or good. For this reason, in Islam the intellect is described as ;*aql -nâqis*, the deficient intellect. The perfection of the intellect is achieved through accepting one's own inadequacy and adhering to the Revelation, which is a means of compensation. It is only possible through *taslîmiyyah*, total reliance on Allah. The intellect is a great blessing from Allah Almighty. But this blessing only gains significance through the Qur'ân and *Sunnah*. Otherwise, the intellect will not prevent its owner from becoming a slave to his *nafs* and drifting towards destruction.

Mawlânâ compares the universe of events ('âlam al-wuqû') to an ocean, and describes mankind as a weak swimmer who is bound to drown. Defying *qadar* by relying on human intellect and volition (*irâda*) is nothing but folly, because unless the intellect and volition submit to *qadar*, that is, fully submit to the will of Allah, no good will come of them.

The precise meaning of *qadar* is unknown. Accordingly, the only way to salvation is to submit to *qadar* after using *irâda,* with recourse to every cause in proportion to one's own capability.

Not only is it useless to wait for the growth of plants before sowing the seed, thinking that merely scattering the seeds is enough for growth is also a vain hope. Scattering seeds is a human task while giving life to the plant is bound to the discretion and might of Allah. For this reason a human "takes recourse to the causes" by sowing the seed and after this "shows reliance and total submission" to the Lord of the Universe, the Controller of *qadar* and all things that occur, and in matters that are beyond us, such as the wind, rain, time and so forth.

The Mathnawi: *"Divine love is like a ship for the distinguished believers. Those who board the ship do not face great calamities or catastrophes, and most often they reach salvation."*

"O You who is travelling to al-Haqq (the Real)! Trade intellect for adoration! Because having intellect is about having an idea and being carried away by speculation!, Whereas adoration is about seeing the beauty, the power and art of Allah, and in being at the end of one's wits."

"Sacrifice intellect in the presence of the honoured Mustafa (*) and say 'Allah is enough for me!'"* (v.4: 1406-1408)

"Intellect and intelligence will bring conceit and arrogance to you." (v.4: 1421)

"Sacrifice the intellect for the love of the true friend! Because all intellect is with the true friend and because all souls and intellect began from Allah. For this reason sacrifice the intellect for the love of Allah."

"Those with intellect have sent it to the place of the true beloved, to the beyond. The intellect that has stayed in this world is the one ignorant of love, one that does not love and is not loved in return, the foolish one." (v. 4: 1424-1425)

As we have mentioned in the explanation of the verses above, using the intellect correctly is only possible if one can understand its compatibility with Divine wisdom and benefit (*maslaha*); that is, the intellect should work in the boundaries of Quran and Sunnah. Thinking that *intellect* has boundless power in understanding everything is as foolish as comparing the power of an ant to a horse.

By saying *"Sacrifice 'aql in the presence of the honoured Mustafa (ﷺ)"* Mawlânâ states the importance of submission to the Divine orders that came through the Prophet (ﷺ). Unless the 'aql is curbed – like a fierce horse- with the reins of the revelation, it will drag its owner to unlimited and boundless pretences, and as a result of this, to destruction.

If a human uses his intellect seeing the wonders of God's creation with the feelings of "adoration", which are the reasons for being aware of Allah Almighty's divine art and power in the universe, they will have perfect faith, "iman al-kamil". Likewise, such a person will be very aware of the inadequacy of their intellect.

However, those who become unequivocally entranced by this adoration become majzoob (one who loses the ability to use their reason because of the love they feel for Allah) due to the fact that they loose their control. Despite wonder and adoration are blessed states, this state is rejected because it constitutes a weakness for the common necessities of human life. For this reason, it is much worthier and desirable to become a jazib who has completed their path rather than becoming a majzoob. Similarly, one who is a jazib is also one of those who have been absorbed in wonder and adoration, who have reached the ruling that says "Allah is sufficient for His servant". In addition to this, a jazib is one who has been able to protect their deliberation. The kind of love and istigraq[21] is seen worthy by Mawlânâ without doubt is the love without loosing the control of the mind.

The Mathnawi: *"What happiness there is for those who see their nafs as wretched! Woe to those who see themselves as superior as the mountains."*

"Know this! Arrogance, sublimeness and seeing oneself superior to others are lethal poison. Fools become intoxicated by drinking this poisonous wine." (v.4: 2746-2747)

A believer needs to don the crown of modesty, and regard his *nafs* as inadequate, even if he possesses many virtues. Those who see themselves as perfect do not try to correct their shortcomings and do not accept their faults. Sufism is the pursuit only of those who have realized their faults and who protect themselves from boasting. The following *hadîth* is pertinent:

"Whoever shows a degree of humility for the sake of Allah, Allah will raise him a degree. Whoever shows arrogance against Allah, Allah will lower him a degree for this, and in the end throw him together with the lowest of the low" (Ibn Mâjah, *Zuhd*, 16)

In the following verse, humble people are praised by Allah and described as follows:

"And the servants of (Allah) Most Gracious are those who walk on the earth in humility, and when the ignorant address them, they say «Peace!»" (Furqân, 25: 63)

In other verses, mankind is ordered to forsake arrogance and boasting:

---

21. One who is submerged in Allah Almighty's ashq to the extent that they forget everything else

"Nor walk on the earth with insolence: for thou canst not rend the earth asunder, nor reach the mountains in height."
(Isrâ', 17: 37)

"And swell not thy cheek (for pride) at men nor walk in insolence through the earth; for Allah loveth not any arrogant boaster." (Luqmân, 31: 18)

One should be mindful that, although humility is a virtue, it should not be a reason for disregarding the blessings of Allah. The point here is the discernment of attributing everything to Allah along with the perception of the blessing itself. In religion, this is known as *tahadduth al-ni'mah*, that is to perceive the existence of the blessings by attributing them to Allah and being thankful for them. This is not arrogance. Arrogance is presuming that a given blessing is from one's *nafs*, to regard it as being from oneself. It is this ego that caused Qârûn to be driven to destruction by his whims and buried into the ground. So, everything that is mentioned by Mawlânâ about *the* intellect, volition, humility and arrogance should be viewed on the grounds of these rational bases.

The Mathnawi: *"Khidr made a hole in the ship and disabled it in order to protect it against some wicked people."*

"Considering that those who are broken, ruined and poor are saved, you too should be among the broken and ruined. Deliverance and security comes with non-existence. Come on, rescue yourself from the nafs and existence, go towards non-existence."

"A mountain that has some gold or silver in it will be smashed to bits with the wounds made by a pickaxe."

"The sword will cut the neck of the person with a neck.

Whereas the shadow is spread out on the ground. There is no wounding it or cutting it because it has neither a neck nor a body." (v.4: 2756-2759)

In the above verses Mawlânâ explains the same reality from different perspectives. Those who are arrogant stir the appetite of others and incite their enmity because they boast about their own merits constantly, ascribe things to themselves with exaggeration. In a famous proverb it is said: *"Whatever a nightingale suffers is because of its voice"*. This means that if the nightingale did not have such a beautiful song no one would put it in a cage. A crow is never kept in a cage.

Thus, we should state that it is merely a rule of this world that a person with merit has enemies, even if that person is like the Prophets, who only have attributes of perfection.

The Mathnawi: *"O heedless ones that struggle for the possessions of this world and who worship it. You also fully possess the wicked immorality of the Pharaoh. You are arrogant, you are full of yourself and you run after possessions and lust! However, your dragon, which is your nafs, has fallen into the pit of feebleness and poverty. It is weak so it cannot attack like the Pharaoh, it cannot do anything."*

"Shame on you! All that has been said are your attributes, your wicked temperament. And you dare to ascribe them to the Pharaoh!"

"Whereas when your bad habits and wicked nature are the subject matter you are annoyed, you do not like it. When the subject is another, it sounds like a tale to you" (vol. 3: 971-973)

Every person has inclinations to both egoistic (*nafsâniyyah*) and spiritual (*ruhâniyyah*) directions. Allah Almighty says in the Qur'ân:

151

"And a soul and Him Who perfected it. And inspired it (with conscience of) what is wrong for it and (what is) right for it." (Shams, 91: 7-8)

Transgression and piety are always in a state that whispers to man and inspires him. For this reason man is like a battlefield and there is a constant conflict between egoistic inclinations, which impels one towards evil, and spiritual inclinations, which impels one towards good.

It is accepted that when a human being conquers his *nafs* unconditionally he will be considered superior to the angels. However, if he succumbs to his *nafs* he will be considered lesser than an animal (*bal hum adal*)[22]. This condition of, being superior to the angels, is due to the fact that angels are not confronted by any obstacle such as the *nafs* when turn towards Allah in worship, as opposed to human beings who do have to overcome such ghastly obstacles. As such, every person inclines towards becoming a "pharaoh". Everyone's circumstances and means differ, so in some these inclinations are as small as buds, whereas in others, with the opportunities that arise, this inclination becomes overbearing and develops into enormous proportions.

Pointing to this fine trait, Mawlânâ Rûmî does not want people who make the Pharaoh a target for the arrows of their criticism and condemnation to forget that they have a lesser pharaoh within themselves. Because this lesser pharaoh has remained in its shell, it has not been able to reach the perfection of the circumstances of the famous historical Pharaoh. If this lesser Pharaoh were to find the circumstances to flourish, it

---

22.   This is a reference to the verse, "[The disbelievers] are like cattle, nay, they are more misguided than cattle".

would not lag behind the real Pharaoh who was determined in his oppression and ego.

In this regard, Rûmî points out that those who criticise others too often fool themselves into thinking that their *nafs* is above such criticism and he says that this situation arises from arrogance.

In another couplet, reiterating the same point, Rûmî says:

"Arrogance, seeing oneself above others, constantly pursues a position, a rank, riches and possessions; because the rich are those who carry dung to heat the furnace of the bath withal.

These two nannies, rank and riches, fatten and thicken the hide and fill it with fat, meat, arrogance and pride."

The Mathnawi: *"Satan is the guide, the leader on the path of arrogance, because he is the first one to fall into and get caught in the trap of worldly position?"*

"This curse is the curse of Satan, Satan was overtaken by his own ego and said, "I have more good than him." In truth, this illness is within every creation, in the nafs of every human being." (v.1: 3216)

"O the person who is hiding the ills of the ego under the curtains of humility and modesty! If someone were to make you angry, stir you and agitate you, just like the water that has filth in it, the colour of filth will come out in the open." (v. 1: 3218)

Among creation, only humans and the jinn are equipped with a *nafs*. According to a well-known opinion, Shaytân, before he rebelled against Allah, was the teacher of angels, but because he was from the lineage of the jinn, he possessed a *nafs*. For this reason, while the angels abided by Allah's command without hesitation when they were ordered to prostrate before Adam, Shaytân claimed that being created from fire meant he was superior to Adam, who had been created from earth. So, he abstained from prostrating and rebelled against Allah. Yet Allah did not ask Shaytân who was superior.

Allah Almighty wanted Shaytân to obey His command to prostrate, but, disregarding this order, Shaytân went on to make a comparison. If we look for a way to avoid the clear decrees of Allah Almighty, if we call upon the feeble resorts of our intellect to set aside these decrees and prohibitions, we will fall into the same calamity and catastrophe that Shaytân did. Those who earn money through interest (ribâ) saying, "I want to become rich with this and do many good things with the money" are an example of this.

As mentioned above, because Shaytân is the first example of one caught up by the *nafs*, the first to oppose Allah due to arrogance, when this is the source of action then it is attributed to Shaytân and referred to as an *Action of Shaytân*. Rûmî considers those who turn away from Allah because of their arrogance to be the subjects of Shaytân. Those who are overtaken by the sin which caused the downfall of Shaytân cannot be saved from being rejected and cursed by Allah.

The Bewilderment
of Pride

THE BEWILDERMENT OF PRIDE

A tiny mouse caught the bridle of an enormous camel, and taking up the reins of the camel he proudly walked in front of the camel. Due to his mild nature the camel just continued to walk as if nothing had happened, and the mouse, unaware of his own insignificance, said: "What a great, strong creature I am. I am even brave enough to drive camels!"

On their way they came to a river. Seeing the river, the tiny proud mouse froze in terror. Aware of the mouse's pride the camel said: "O you who have kept me company in the meadows and through the mountains! Why have you stopped? Why are you so surprised? Go on, jump into the river; with all your courage, are you not my leader and guide? Is it better to stop like this in the middle of the road?"

The mouse, embarrassed, answered, stuttering: "My friend! This river is so big and deep that I am afraid I will drown." The camel went into the water and said: "O, blind mouse! The water is only knee high; there is nothing to be afraid of!" Having no choice, the mouse confessed: "O, camel! The river may be like an ant to you, but to me it is a great monster. The height of everyone's knees is different; if we were to put one hundred of my legs, one on top of the other, then they would barely reach your knee."

After hearing this, the clever camel gave the mouse some advice: "In that case, do not be misled by your pride and arrogance; do not treat others rudely and know your place! Do not be misled by the gentleness I have shown you, because Allah does not like the proud ones! Go and take on mice of your own size!" The mouse now understood his error and was very ashamed. He said: "I am sorry for what I have done! I will never do it again, but please, take me across this deadly river!" The camel said to him: "Come on! Jump onto my hump! Taking you across this river is my job. My duty is to help thousands of helpless ones like you." The camel took the mouse over the river.

In this story told by Mawlânâ Rûmî, the mouse represents those people who try to take on things that are too great for them to handle; the mouse is proud and thinks that he is better than everyone else, while the camel is the symbol of a patient, wise, clever and mature person. The purpose of this story is to convey wisdom, examples of opinions, thoughts and feelings. The following lines show us the great wisdom here:

"At first the devil was seen as a great being among the angels, and he became accustomed to this, thinking that he was better than every other being. Due to this he became spoiled and was unaware of the magnificence inherent in the commands of Allah Almighty. He saw Prophet Adam (upon him be peace) as being inferior and despicable; so Iblis was afflicted with the worst possible fate."

"Copper does not realize it is copper until it becomes gold. The heart does not realize its mistakes or understand its inferiority until it attains a certain spiritual consistency. O soul! Save your ego from the dungeons of arrogance and pride and serve the potion of life so that you can become gold! Serve it with heartfelt love…"

"These lovers are those that have souls; just as the day and night avoid one another, so too do they avoid the world, and without never inclining to it!"

All this shows that whenever pretension or selfishness enters the heart, an idolatry of degree and rank sets in motion; in such a heart there can never be compassion because pretension and selfishness are the cancer of spiritual life. The cause of pretension and selfishness is a person's conceit before the Divine power. Even though we are nothing more than a tiny grain of sand in an enormous desert, we forget our limitations and are deceived by a little praise and some opportunities, and then perceive ourselves as being above others; this is nothing but conceit.

Without a doubt, pride makes a person perceive of themselves as having more power, talent and ability than they really do. But is not the power of all living creatures the very power with which Allah Almighty has blessed them? Shame on those who are unaware of this reality! The pride of Pharaoh and Nimrod led them to claim divinity; as a result they were punished by Divine retribution. This is why Prophet Muhammad (ﷺ), particularly after great victories, would always counsel the Companions with submission and humility and prevent them from boasting. At the Battle of Badr, a triumph in the struggle for Islam, first a thousand, then three thousand and finally five thousand angels, according to the level of faith of the believers, were sent to their aid. Allah declared in the Qur'ân:

"...When thou threw (a handful) of (dust), it was not thy act, but Allah's!..." (Anfâl, 8: 17)

The Prophet and his Companions are eternal examples for all of mankind as a result of such behavior. At the conquest of Mecca, the Prophet Muhammad actually conquered hearts rather than the city. On entering that holy city there were no indications of a victory; in fact, Prophet Muhammad (ﷺ) bowed on his camel in prostration, overcome by a feeling of gratitude to Allah. All such situations contain principles. For this reason it is said: *'Whoever knows his nafs (self) knows his Lord'*

Mawlânâ Rûmî warns people: "O heedless man! As you are not a messenger you cannot be aware of what is beyond and nobody will follow you: know your place on this path then and follow your own line, do not go any further! Walk behind a great guardian on the path of truth that you are following so that one day you will emerge from the well of egoism and be a sultan of sense, like Prophet Yusuf."

"Since you have neither the immortality of the Almighty, nor the language of the Almighty, then listen! If you will say something then say it as if it is a question so that the words will benefit and you can learn something! Speak to the Sultan of the sultans like a poor and needy man!"

"The beginning of pride and resentment is an extreme love for all egoistical desires, richness and worldly cravings. These extreme desires are embedded in the soul to become habit! When bad habits are strengthened, you abuse those who try to make you abandon the habits and you feel resentment towards them. Even idol worshippers make worshipping the idols a habit; they become enemies of those who try to prevent them from doing so."

May Allah protect us from conceit and the confusion of pride and arrogance and place us among those who know themselves, who are aware of themselves, the good ones who spend their lives worshipping the Creator!

Âmîn!